RIGHTEOUS
WARRIORS

RIGHTEOUS WARRIORS

Lessons from the War Chapters in the Book of Mormon

JOHN BYTHEWAY

DESERET
BOOK

SALT LAKE CITY, UTAH

Library of Congress Cataloging-in-Publication Data

Bytheway, John, 1962-
  Righteous warriors : lessons from the war chapters in the Book of Mormon / John Bytheway.
      p. cm.
  Includes bibliographical references and index.
  ISBN 1-59038-271-4 (pbk. : alk. paper)
  1. Mormon youth—Religious life. 2. Book of Mormon. Alma XLIII-LXII—Criticism, interpretation, etc. I. Title.
  BX8643.Y6B9655 2004
  289.3'22—dc22
                                        2004000910

Printed in the United States of America   18961-040P
R.R. Donnelley and Sons, Crawfordsville, IN

10   9   8   7   6   5   4   3   2   1

JACK LEE BYTHEWAY, 1926–2004

To my dad,
a Righteous Warrior
who fought a good fight,
finished his course,
and kept the faith

CONTENTS

ACKNOWLEDGMENTS

I wish to thank Robert L. Millet, who encouraged me to turn these ideas into a book. I'd also like to thank S. Michael Wilcox and M. Todd Murdock for their insights on the war chapters.

I am grateful to the staff at Deseret Book for their careful and professional work. I am particularly grateful to Michael Morris for his editing skills and helpful suggestions, Tom Hewitson for the beautiful cover design, and Susan Dayley for her comments and ideas.

I am most thankful for the constant support of my wife, Kimberly, who read the initial manuscript and offered valuable help and suggestions.

In the Church we are not neutral. We are one-sided. There is a war going on, and we are engaged in it. It is the war between good and evil, and we are belligerents defending the good. We are therefore obliged to give preference to and protect all that is represented in the gospel of Jesus Christ, and we have made covenants to do it.

—BOYD K. PACKER, *MEMORABLE STORIES AND PARABLES BY BOYD K. PACKER* (SALT LAKE CITY: BOOKCRAFT, 1997), 23.

INTRODUCTION

Why are there so many wars in the Book of Mormon? That's a good question, and there are several good answers. We know that the Book of Mormon was written for our time and that the ancient prophets saw what life would be like for us in the latter days. Let's think about that for a minute—if they saw our day, what did they see?

Centuries of Conflict

The Book of Mormon was unearthed and translated a few decades after the Revolutionary War and published eighteen years after the War of 1812 (when was that?). The Mormon Battalion went to assist the U.S. Army in the Mexican War in 1846. The Civil War (1861–65) followed fifteen years later, and the Spanish-American War (1898) came three decades after that. World War I (1914–18) was fought during my grandfather's time, and World War II (1941–45) and the Korean War (1950–53) occurred when

1

my dad was young. The Vietnam War (1964–73) happened during my childhood, and we all remember the Persian Gulf War (1991). As I write this chapter at the end of 2003, fighting still rages in the aftermath of the War in Iraq. That's pretty sobering, and those were only some of the wars in which the United States was involved. I didn't mention any of the hundreds of wars fought around the world in the past two hundred years.

So if the ancient prophets saw our day, what would we expect them to write about, peace? No. They saw our day and the wars of our day, so they wrote about war. What would *really* be strange is if we had a book written for our day with no wars in it. (Can you imagine a large part of the Book of Mormon called "the peace chapters"? Can't you just hear some people say, "Hey, why is there so much peace in here?") If the Book of Mormon were warless, how could it help us in our day, which is characterized by war?

The "General" Idea

Perhaps another reason the Book of Mormon includes so many wars is that Mormon, the prophet who abridged it, was a military man himself. He included the things he knew about! He saw gospel principles in the things he experienced, and he shared them with us so that we could see them too. President Boyd K. Packer said Mormon was "not able to resist putting in a generous amount of military science and tactics—for he was a general. This unusual human insight is also a testimony!" (*Let Not Your Heart Be Troubled* [Salt Lake City: Bookcraft, 1991], 276).

It Ain't Over 'Til It's Over

The war chapters were preserved for us because the war that began in heaven, which was a spiritual struggle involving testimony and allegiance to the Father's plan, is continuing here on earth and is far from over. Elder Russell M. Nelson taught:

> We must realize that we are at war. The war began before the world was, and it will continue. The forces of the adversary are extant upon the earth. All of our virtuous motives, if transmitted only by inertia and timidity, are no match for the resolute wickedness of those who oppose us (*The Power within Us* [Salt Lake City: Deseret Book, 1988], 99).

All of these reasons help us understand why the Book of Mormon discusses so many wars. I love the war chapters. I don't love war, but I love these chapters—and I know that I'm not alone. Many of us love the war chapters because of their intriguing mixture of heroism, adventure, treachery, deception, faith, and devotion. We're fascinated by brilliant military tactics using prophetic reconnaissance and by deceptively simple stratagems, decoys, and snares. We're sobered when we see the effects of raw ambition and political upheaval on the children of Lehi. And we're touched by the profound gratitude and deep sorrow among those who are spared in the aftermath.

Perhaps most important, we are reminded that the conflict that began in the premortal existence has simply switched locations. Perhaps we may benefit from the lessons learned long ago by the children of Lehi in their time of war.

In the war chapters we're inspired by the examples of Captain Moroni, Helaman, Teancum, the stripling warriors, and others—towering characters of unwavering commitment and resolute defenders of freedom and liberty. We're taught that their victories did not come because of superior armor, fortifications, or tactics but because of unshakable faith in Christ.

Not only do these chapters give us insights to prepare us for life's never-ending spiritual battles, but they also warn us to beware of the stratagems of the adversary, whose ultimate goal is to bring us into bondage and destruction.

You're Gonna Do *What?*

More than a few people were a bit surprised when I told them I was working on a book for teenagers about the war chapters in the Book of Mormon. *Are you crazy? Are you loco loco? Are you teched in the head?* Yeah, I'm probably a little strange, but I like to react to those questions by sharing what I've learned about LDS teenagers.

A few years ago I was working for the BYU summer camp called Especially for Youth. We decided we wanted to make the scriptures a more fundamental part of the program. In fact we decided we would make the scriptures the "ticket" the youth would need to be admitted to an EFY class. Those who didn't have their ticket couldn't come in. We worried that some might forget to bring their scriptures or say they were too heavy or too inconvenient to carry around campus all day. We even talked about having a box of scriptures at the door of each class for those who forgot to bring their own, but we changed our minds because we didn't want anyone to rely on our extra sets.

We were nervous when the summer sessions began, but we knew our "ticket" idea was the right thing to do. So we told the teenagers that they *had to have their scriptures,* and we waited to see what would happen. The rest is history. We were surprised, we were amazed, and we were impressed. They not only brought their scriptures, but they also opened them and marked them. They also followed along and asked questions. We were excited, and our EFY teachers were thrilled.

I learned on that occasion (and on many other occasions) to never underestimate LDS teenagers. I guess President J. Reuben Clark Jr. was right when he said, "You do not have to sneak up behind this spiritually experienced youth and whisper religion in his ears; you can come right out, face to face, and talk with him" ("The Charted Course of the Church in Education," in Boyd K. Packer, *Teach Ye Diligently* [Salt Lake City: Deseret Book, 1975], 317).

President Gordon B. Hinckley has also commented on today's teenagers and their familiarity with the scriptures:

> I look back to my own youth. Neither young men nor young women were doing much scripture reading at that time. What a marvelous change has been wrought. A new generation is arising who are familiar with the word of the Lord. . . . I meet young people everywhere who are wonderful and faithful; youth who want to do the right thing and who indicate the reality of what I have been saying for a long time,

that we've never had a better generation of young people in the Church than we have today. They are faithful. They are active. They're knowledgeable. They are a great generation, notwithstanding the environment in which many of them are growing up (Gordon B. Hinckley, *Teachings of Gordon B. Hinckley* [Salt Lake City: Deseret Book, 1997], 714–15).

So I'm not worried. In fact, I'm excited to write about these interesting chapters, and I'm looking forward to taking this journey with you. I love the scriptures, and there isn't anything I'd rather talk about. So this book involves two of my favorite things: the Book of Mormon and teenagers.

We're Going In . . .

I hope you will want to highlight some scriptures in your Book of Mormon as you go through these chapters, but I also know that it's difficult to have two books open at the same time unless you're sitting at a table. And since teenagers rarely read at tables, I'm going to try to retell the story line of each chapter while we look for the lessons— things that we can apply to our own lives. To help you get the story line in your head, I've included the synopsis from the Book of Mormon (the small italicized paragraph that precedes each chapter) at the beginning of each chapter in this book.

So here's the plan: We're going to go through Alma 43–62 and look for the spiritual lessons. As I studied the war chapters, every once in a while I had to stop, get out my red pencil, and say, "Hmmm, that's interesting." Other times it was more like, "Wow, there's an insight." And here and there I got a "Whoa, that's a major lesson!" So that's what I did as I wrote about these chapters. I paused in the story line, indented a paragraph here and there, and labeled it like this:

➤ **Observation**—For the "Hmmm, that's interesting" parts

≈ **Mini Lesson**—For the "Wow, there's an insight" parts

❧ **Major Lesson**—For the "Whoa, that's a major lesson!" parts

You'll probably discover many of your own observations, insights, and lessons as well—that's what makes scripture reading so interesting! It's like a puzzle that is never completely solved or a "find the hidden objects" drawing with hundreds of treasures concealed inside. The objects are there for everyone to discover, but they're difficult to see except for those who study and search again and again.

Enemies of Captain Moroni

Before we get under way it might be helpful to divide the war chapters into more manageable parts. As you know, the central character of the war chapters is Captain Moroni. Moroni faces many foes in these chapters, ranging as we sometimes say "from A to Z" (although in reality they go from "Z to A"). I like to divide the war chapters into four sections based on Moroni's adversaries.

1. Captain Moroni vs. Zerahemnah: Alma 43–44
2. Captain Moroni vs. Amalickiah: Alma 46–51

3. Captain Moroni vs. Ammoron: Alma 52–58
4. Captain Moroni vs. the king-men in Zarahemla: Alma 51, 59–62

Captain Moroni first faced Zerahemnah. Then he had to deal with Amalickiah, who was succeeded by his brother, Ammoron. Later Moroni had to return to Zarahemla and contend with the king-men.

➡ **Observation:** What all these enemies had in common, oddly enough, is that they were all Nephites. The Lamanites provided the bulk of the armies but only after they had been stirred up to anger by these apostate Nephites! Most Nephite difficulties, therefore, were caused not by Lamanites but by their own people! (We find parallels to this situation in early Church history as we recall the friends of Joseph Smith who apostatized from the Church and became bitter enemies and persecutors). It's also worth noting that all of these enemies set out to destroy the liberty and freedom of the Nephites. We see in these chapters the continuing struggle between agency and bondage that began with the war in heaven. ◄

At the conclusion of the war chapters, Captain Moroni retired to his home, and his responsibilities passed to his son, Moronihah. The enemies of Captain Moroni had either taken oaths not to fight or had been destroyed or driven out of Nephite lands. When peace finally returned to the Nephites, Captain Moroni was still around—a powerful testimony to the faith, brilliance, and competence of this hero of the Book of Mormon.

CHAPTER 1

ALMA 43

Prophets Know Where the Enemy Will Strike

Alma and his sons preach the word—The Zoramites and other Nephite dissenters become Lamanites—The Lamanites come against the Nephites in war—Moroni arms the Nephites with defensive armor—The Lord reveals to Alma the strategy of the Lamanites—The Nephites defend their homes, liberties, families, and religion—The armies of Moroni and Lehi surround the Lamanites (ALMA 43 HEADNOTE).

As we begin the first of the war chapters, we learn that "the Zoramites became Lamanites" (Alma 43:4). How does a Zoramite "become" a Lamanite? Did they "white out" their pedigree charts and stop showing up at family reunions? No. Obviously the Zoramites didn't change their *genealogy;* rather, they changed their *beliefs!*

➡ **Observation:** As we go through the Book of Mormon we begin to notice that over time the difference between the Nephites and the Lamanites is more and more a matter of affiliation and belief and less and less a matter of lineage and birth. Later we'll point out a few exceptions, but for the most part, the Nephites believe in God, and the Lamanites are either apostates or do not know about God. That is why I prefer to call modern-day descendants of those in the Book of Mormon "children of Lehi" rather than "Lamanites." ◄◄

We know that the Zoramites had changed their beliefs because just a few chapters earlier they were praying atop the Rameumptom. They soon joined another group of apostates called the Amalekites, led by a man named Zerahemnah. This is Zerahem-*nah*, not to be confused with Zarahem-*la*. One is a man; the other is a place. (Zarahem-*la* was named after a man, but he was long gone by this time.)

Anyway, Zerahemnah stirred up the Lamanites to anger against the Nephites and appointed chief captains among his apostate Nephite friends to lead an army of Lamanites into battle against the Nephites.

Who Started It?

Mormon wants us to understand why the Lamanites and Nephites are fighting. Here's what he says about the Lamanites: "[Zerahemnah's] designs were to stir up the Lamanites to anger against the Nephites; this he did that he might usurp great power over them, and also that he might gain power over the Nephites by bringing them into bondage" (Alma 43:8).

Here's what he says about the Nephites: "And now the design of the Nephites was to support their lands, and their houses, and their wives, and their children, that they might preserve them from the hands of their enemies; and also that they might preserve their rights and their privileges, yea, and also their liberty, that they might worship God according to their desires" (Alma 43:9).

➡ **Observation:** It's difficult to imagine the emotional and spiritual turmoil experienced by Moroni and his army. These men probably held the priesthood! They were trying to be a light to the world and to love and serve their fellow beings! They would need to know exactly why they were defending themselves, which often involved the gruesome business of taking life. In several places throughout the war chapters, Mormon repeats their reasons for taking up arms. ◀

Mormon tells us that Moroni was appointed chief captain of all the Nephite armies when he was only twenty-five years old (Alma 43:17). This was the same age of Alma the Elder when he defended Abinadi in King Noah's court seventy-four years earlier. I don't know exactly why Mormon mentions Moroni's age, but I'm glad he did! It reminds us that we don't have to be old to be valiant.

You're Not Going Out in *That*, Are You?

When the armies of the Lamanites met the Nephites in the borders of Jershon, the Lamanite armies were afraid. Why? Because the Nephites were equipped with armor—

breastplates, arm-shields, helmets, and thick clothing. The Lamanites had plenty of weapons but no armor—only a "skin which was girded about their loins" (Alma 43:20).

I doubt that any of us would want to go anywhere in a loincloth, and I imagine that going into battle would be one of the least desirable places to be caught in such attire. Can't you just see the Lamanites preparing for battle?

"Let's see. I'm going to fight today. What should I wear? Ah, the loincloth! And some sunscreen. And maybe some extra safety pins."

Just one Nephite with a handful of sharp rocks and a good arm could cause considerable physical discomfort for the Lamanite armies. Predictably, when the armies of the Lamanites saw the Nephites with their armor, the Lamanites had a sudden change of plans and departed for the land of Manti instead.

Notice the brilliance of Captain Moroni in these circumstances: "Moroni sent spies into the wilderness to watch their camp; and Moroni, also, knowing of the prophecies of Alma, sent certain men unto him, desiring him that he should inquire of the Lord whither the armies of the Nephites should go to defend themselves against the Lamanites" (Alma 43:23).

≈ **Mini Lesson:** This is a wonderful illustration of faith and works. You do what you can do, and you ask God to help you with what you cannot do. You send your spies, *and* you ask the prophet for help. Having a prophet is better than having satellite photos or real-time reconnaissance. President Marion G. Romney once remarked that God "can only guide our footsteps when we move our feet" ("Principles of Temporal Salvation," *Ensign*, April 1981, 4). Moroni reminds us of the old saying, "Pray as if everything depended on God, and work as if everything depended on you." Captain Moroni does both. ≈

Moroni was quite a leader, but he was also eager to use and follow the counsel of the prophet. No matter how brilliant or how capable we think we are, if we're wise, we'll always look to the prophet for help in our spiritual battles.

The Threat Board

Another spiritual insight we can gain from this account is this: Prophets know where the enemy will attack and can prepare us to meet the threat!

> ≈ **Mini Lesson:** Modern warships track potential enemies and chart their positions on what is called a "threat board." At any moment the commander of a vessel can discern potential dangers. If we are going to be attacked spiritually in these latter days, how do we prepare? We can be vigilant and we can be aware, but we can also listen to and follow the prophet. Modern prophets can tell us what's on the threat board, and they can tell us exactly where the enemy will strike. ≈

President Harold B. Lee taught, "Satan's greatest *threat* today is to destroy the family, and to make mockery of the law of chastity and the sanctity of the marriage covenant" ("Pres. Lee Speaks," *Church News*, August 19, 1972, 3;

emphasis added). President Lee made that comment more than thirty years ago when the threat was not nearly as obvious as it is now. President Ezra Taft Benson later quoted two prophets in making the following observation:

> The plaguing sin of this generation is sexual immorality. This, the Prophet Joseph said, would be the source of more temptations, more buffetings, and more difficulties for the elders of Israel than any other. (See *Journal of Discourses* 8:55.)
>
> President Joseph F. Smith said that sexual impurity would be one of the three dangers that would *threaten* the Church within—and so it does. . . . It permeates our society (*A Witness and a Warning* [Salt Lake City: Deseret Book, 1988], 74; emphasis added).

Moroni was a brilliant and capable military commander. He must have had a million things on his mind in preparing to defend the Nephites, but he took time to listen to the prophet. If Moroni stopped to listen to the prophet's voice in preparing for his battles, maybe we can take a break twice a year to prepare for our battles by listening to general conference.

There Are Causes, and There Are Better Causes

Using information from the prophet Alma, Moroni concealed his army in various areas so that they surrounded the Lamanites when they approached the borders of the land of Manti. With their backs to the wall and with little opportunity to escape, the Lamanites fought "like dragons," but the

"Nephites were inspired by a better cause, for they were not fighting for monarchy nor power but they were fighting for their homes and their liberties, their wives and their children, and their all, yea, for their rites of worship and their church" (Alma 43:44–45).

> ➵ **Observation:** All decent parents would fight to defend their children from bodily harm, but how hard do we fight against our family's spiritual enemies? The Nephites were engaged in a physical battle to defend their loved ones, and today we're engaged in a spiritual battle to protect our families. Physical enemies threaten the body, but spiritual enemies threaten the soul. ⇠

An enemy has to be recognized before it can be conquered. Today one of the major enemies on the threat board is modern media. This enemy wears many disguises, like "It's just a movie" camouflage or "It's only a CD" fatigues. Media enemies enter our homes through cable, modem, or satellite dish disguised as "harmless entertainment" when, in reality, they are on a covert mission to destroy. Latter-day families have little choice but to confront this enemy because it is so persistent and pervasive. Fortunately we know we're fighting a defensive battle, and we can fight with the confidence that we are inspired "by a better cause."

Mercy or Revenge?

The Nephites repelled the Lamanites' final push, and the armies of the Lamanites fled to the river of Sidon only to see that their escape route had been cut off by the armies of the

Nephites. When Moroni "saw their terror" he "commanded his men that they should stop shedding their blood"—a clear evidence of Moroni's merciful nature (Alma 43:54).

Can you imagine the drama of the moment at the end of Alma 43? The fighting had ceased, and the Lamanite armies were in Moroni's hands. Moroni was surrounded by fallen and wounded Nephites who had fought to protect their families and their right to worship God as they chose. Did the sight of his own people among the dead fill Moroni with anger and revenge? Did the thought of returning home to face the widows and children of these valiant defenders make Moroni want to finish the job against the Lamanites?

Amid the blood and carnage, youthful Captain Moroni stood face-to-face with Zerahemnah, who was in his hands and at his mercy. Wouldn't we have empathized with Moroni had he wanted to wipe the Lamanites off the face of the earth forever? We'll see what happens in the next chapter.

Lessons from Alma 43

1. The Lord is concerned with the desires of our hearts (why we do what we do).
2. Faith and works: We do what we can do, and the Lord will help us with the rest.
3. The prophets know where the enemy will strike, so listen up!

CHAPTER 2

ALMA 44

Faith in Christ in
Times of War and Peace

*Moroni commands the Lamanites to make a covenant of peace
or be destroyed—Zerahemnah rejects the offer, and the battle
resumes—Moroni's armies defeat the Lamanites* (ALMA 44
HEADNOTE).

Zerahemnah and his armies were surrounded. Captain
Moroni, backed by a well-equipped army with God on its side,
cut off the Lamanites' escape route. But Moroni was not a man
who delighted in bloodshed. Just imagine the scene! Leaders
of opposing armies standing face-to-face, the roar of battle suddenly replaced by the relative silence of a truce. Perhaps young
Captain Moroni removed his helmet, "withdrew a pace," and
prepared to speak. No paraphrase of mine can hope to match
the power of Moroni's words direct from the scriptures:

> Behold, Zerahemnah, that we do not desire to be
> men of blood. Ye know that ye are in our hands, yet
> we do not desire to slay you.

17

Behold, we have not come out to battle against you that we might shed your blood for power; neither do we desire to bring any one to the yoke of bondage. But this is the very cause for which ye have come against us; yea, and ye are angry with us because of our religion.

But now, ye behold that the Lord is with us; and ye behold that he has delivered you into our hands. And now I would that ye should understand that this is done unto us because . . . (Alma 44:1–3).

Forgive the interruption, but what will Moroni say next? What will he offer as the sole reason for his army's success? Will he boast of his superior military strategy? Will he take credit for the skill and advanced tactics of his army? Will he mock the Lamanites for showing up so underdressed? No.

Faith in Christ

Captain Moroni never took credit for success and always took responsibility for failure. Surely Moroni was aware of the counsel of Alma the Elder to "stand as witnesses of God at all times and in all things, and in all places" (Mosiah 18:9). That includes times of war. Moroni continued:

And now I would that ye should understand that this is done unto us because of our religion and our *faith in Christ*. And now ye see that ye cannot destroy this our *faith*. Now ye see that this is the true *faith* of God; yea, ye see that God will support, and keep, and preserve us, so long as we are *faithful* unto him, and unto our *faith*, and our religion; and never

18

will the Lord suffer that we shall be destroyed except we should fall into transgression and deny our *faith* (Alma 44:3–4; emphasis added).

When I talk about the war chapters in a fireside setting, I have the youth snap their fingers whenever they hear the word *faith*. Go back and try it. You'll notice that the verses above contain the word "faith," or "faithful" six times!

❧ **Major Lesson:** Wow! If faith in Jesus Christ really is the first principle of the gospel, then it is the first principle of the gospel even in war. Faith in Jesus Christ is power in times of prosperity and power in times of trial. It will see us through our minor daily struggles and our major spiritual battles. Here's a great statement from Elder M. Russell Ballard:

"Faith in the Lord Jesus Christ is a power to be reckoned with in the universe and in individual lives. It can be a causative force through which miracles are wrought. It can also be a source of inner strength through which we find self-esteem, peace of mind, contentment, and the courage to cope. I have seen marriages saved, families strengthened, tragedies overcome, careers energized, and the will to go on living rekindled as people humble themselves before the Lord and accept His will in their lives. Heartache, tragedy, and trauma of all kinds can be focused and managed when the principles of the gospel of Jesus Christ are understood and applied" (*Our Search for Happiness: An Invitation to Understand The Church of Jesus Christ of Latter-day Saints* [Salt Lake City: Deseret Book, 1993], 15–16).

So how do you handle life when it gets tough? *Faith in Christ!* The Savior knows how tough life can be. How do you handle life when problems arise in your family? *Faith in Christ!* He knows how to heal hearts. How do you handle life when you have no friends or when your friends desert you? *Faith in Christ!* Jesus knows what it's like to feel wrongly accused, misunderstood, and betrayed. And because he knows those things, he can help you through similar experiences.

When I was in college, I labeled a page in my planner "Quotes on Faith and Hope." Whenever I felt discouraged or doubtful, I'd open to that page and read those quotes to myself. Two verses on that page always helped me to keep the faith: "All flesh is in mine hands; be still and know that I am God" (D&C 101:16), and "Therefore, fear not, little flock; do good; let earth and hell combine against you, for if ye are built upon my rock, they cannot prevail" (D&C 6:34). ◈

At All Times

Okay, back to the story. In his testimony to Zerahemnah and his army, Moroni could have said, "Drop your weapons, swear an oath, and return to your lands, or we will destroy you." After all, what good is bearing your testimony to hardened apostates who had the truth and turned against it? But perhaps Moroni wasn't talking to Zerahemnah or the other apostate Nephites—maybe he was bearing his testimony to the Lamanite armies! Or perhaps he was thinking of the impact his testimony might have had on his own men.

Or maybe he wasn't thinking any of those things. I suspect that Captain Moroni didn't feel any need to "weigh his words" or "figure out his audience" because he was a witness of God, and he would bear his witness at all times, in all things, and in all places. Before Moroni delivered his terms of surrender, he commanded Zerahemnah in the name of God and listed other reasons for which the Nephites were fighting.

> And now, Zerahemnah, I command you, in the name of that all-powerful God, who has strengthened our arms that we have gained power over you, by our faith, by our religion, and by our rites of worship, and by our church, and by the sacred support which we owe to our wives and our children, by that liberty which binds us to our lands and our country; yea, and also by the maintenance of the sacred word of God, to which we owe all our happiness; and by all that is most dear unto us (Alma 44:5).

I think it's pretty rare to be able to fight in the name of God. Too many wars in world history have been fought in his name but without his endorsement. Moroni had the Lord's endorsement and could command in his name. When we ponder Moroni's success, we're reminded of the faith-building statement of Paul: "If God be for us, who can prevail against us?" (JST, Romans 8:31).

Worth Fighting For

Among the other things the Nephites were fighting for, Moroni mentioned "the sacred support which we owe to our wives and our children." There were no deadbeat dads in this group. Imagine what a different world we would have if all fathers felt that kind of responsibility. Moroni also commanded Zerahemnah by "the maintenance of the sacred word of God, to which we owe all our happiness" (Alma 44:5).

➡ **Observation:** What do you think members of the Church would answer if you asked them, "To what do you owe all your happiness?" Their possessions? Their friends? Their fame or popularity? I know people who have all of those things and still aren't happy. How would the Book of Mormon answer that question? Well, in the vision of the tree of life, the rod of iron was the word of God that led to the fruit of the tree, which was desirable to "make one happy" (1 Nephi 8:10). We may search if we wish, but we will ultimately discover that there is no substitute tree of life. Nothing else in Lehi's vision even compared with the love of God. (Perhaps there were vending machines in the great and spacious building, but what they offered was nutritionally worthless.) The greatest joy, the most satisfying food to the soul, the most desirable thing in this life (and in the next) is the fruit of the tree of life. And the only way to get to that fruit is by holding fast to the rod of iron, or, in

22

Moroni's words, "the sacred word of God, to which we owe all our happiness." ◄═

After Moroni commanded in the name of God and "by all that [was] most dear unto" the Nephites, he dictated his benevolent terms of surrender: "I command you by all the desires which ye have for life, that ye deliver up your weapons of war unto us, and we will seek not your blood, but we will spare your lives, if ye will go your way and come not again to war against us" (Alma 44:6). Moroni was only twenty-five, but his respect for the lives of enemy attackers, his extension of mercy when mercy was undeserved, and his self-control in the midst of war were amazing.

Zerahemnah agreed that his men would deliver up their weapons, but he refused to take an oath "which we know that we shall break, and also our children." Predictably, Zerahemnah didn't believe that faith in God had anything to do with the Nephite army's success. Rather, he said, "It is your cunning" and "your breastplates and your shields that have preserved you" (Alma 44:8, 9).

Following Zerahemnah's refusal to depart with an oath of peace, Moroni, in a moment of great faith and courage, returned Zerahemnah's weapons and declared, "Behold, we will end the conflict." Moroni did not compromise with evil. Either Zerahemnah did things God's way, or he would be destroyed (which is what happens to all who fail to follow God). There were no discussions, no bipartisan agreements, no negotiations.

Zerahemnah, in a fit of anger, then rushed forward to slay Moroni. But as he raised his sword, one of Moroni's soldiers struck it and broke it at the hilt. He then turned his sword on Zerahemnah and "took off his scalp" (Alma 44:10, 12).

Placing the scalp on the point of his sword for all to see, the soldier offered a little object lesson:

> Even as this scalp has fallen to the earth, which is the scalp of your chief, so shall ye fall to the earth except ye will deliver up your weapons of war and depart with a covenant of peace (Alma 44:14).

When they saw Zerahemnah's scalp clinging to the point of a sword, many in the Lamanite army thought, "Hmmm, that's a pretty impressive object lesson—I surrender." They then departed with an oath. But others remained to fight, and the battle resumed. Finally, Zerahemnah (who somehow continued to fight without his scalp) "saw that they were all about to be destroyed," and he "cried mightily unto Moroni, promising that he [and his people] would covenant" never to come again to war against the Nephites (Alma 44:19).

Keeping Covenants

Moroni could have said, "I'm sorry, you had your chance," but instead he called another cease-fire, and that's how the battle ended. No malice, no retribution, no trials for war crimes—Moroni simply let the Lamanites return to the wilderness after they made a covenant of peace.

> ➡ **Observation:** We know that in ancient times an oath was a powerful and binding commitment, even among the wicked. If Godless apostates like

24

Zerahemnah can keep their covenants, maybe we can keep ours. ◄━

Well, Zerahemnah was gone. Not Zarahem-*la* but Zeraham-*nah*, as in the song heard when someone fouls out in a basketball game: "Nah-nah-nah-nah, nah-nah-nah-nah, hey-hey-hey, good-bye."

What did it cost the Nephites to defend their families, their rights, and their freedoms? Alma 44 concludes, "Now the number of their dead was not numbered because of the greatness of the number; yea, the number of their dead was exceedingly great, both on the Nephites and on the Lamanites" (Alma 44:21). Faith in Christ triumphs, as it always does, but truly, as the bumper sticker on the back of my truck suggests, "Freedom isn't free."

Many Nephites had died defending their families and freedoms, and many more would die. If you knew that more wars were coming, how would you prepare your people? What would you do first? Those are the questions we'll answer next as we look at Alma 45.

Lessons from Alma 44

1. Faith in Jesus Christ is powerful in any situation.
2. A testimony can be shared in unusual places, even in war.
3. We owe all of our happiness to the word of God.
4. If warring apostates can keep covenants, maybe we can keep ours.

CHAPTER 3

ALMA 45

Expedient to Declare
the Word of God

Helaman believes the words of Alma—Alma prophesies the destruction of the Nephites—He blesses and curses the land—Alma is taken up by the Spirit, even as Moses—Dissension grows in the Church (ALMA 45 HEADNOTE).

Okay, this chapter is fairly short. Here's the scoop: After being delivered out of the hands of Zerahemnah, the people of Nephi fasted and prayed in gratitude and worshiped God "with exceedingly great joy." Alma the Younger blessed his son Helaman, prophesied the ultimate destruction of the Nephites, departed out of the land, and "was never heard of more" (Alma 45:1, 18). Helaman, as the new leader of the Church, looked upon the Nephites and their war-torn society. What should he do?

Jesus said that man should not live by bread alone, but by *words*—every word that comes from the mouth of God (Matthew 4:4). Hmmm, bread and words. We might say that the most important thing next to food is words! And we can back that up. Nephi and his brothers returned to Jerusalem to obtain the brass plates, which became a stabilizing force for the Nephites for many centuries.

Have a Nice Trip and Don't Forget to Pack Your Words!

Do you remember earlier in the Book of Mormon when the first King Mosiah led his people out of the land of Nephi and discovered the people of Zarahem-*la*? The people of Zarahemla, also known as Mulekites, were a group of Israelites that had left Jerusalem about the same time as Lehi. The Mulekites had taken bread on their journey but no words of God! Without God's words, their society and their spirituality had fallen apart! When King Mosiah found them, "their language had become corrupted; and they had brought no records with them; and they denied the being of their Creator; and Mosiah, nor the people of Mosiah, could understand them" (Omni 1:17).

Thus the "word of God" can be a unifying, civilizing force for mankind. Helaman knew this and began to use the word of God to rebuild and strengthen his country:

> For behold, because of the wars with the Lamanites and the many little dissensions and disturbances which had been among the people, it became expedient that the word of God should be declared among them, yea, and that a regulation should be made throughout the church (Alma 45:21).

Helaman's plan for rebuilding the land and the people was not focused on their cities, forts, or infrastructure. It was to declare the word of God. This, of course, is not the only instance in the Book of Mormon that the word of God was seen as the cure for a weakened society. Notice footnote "a" in Alma 45:21, which takes us to Alma 31:5. Here we see the tool that Alma used to reclaim the Zoramites:

> And now, as *the preaching of the word* had a great tendency to lead the people to do that which was just—yea, it had had more powerful effect upon the minds of the people than the sword, or anything else, which had happened unto them—therefore Alma thought it was expedient that they should try the virtue of the word of God (emphasis added).

It wasn't bread the people needed most, it was words—the words of God.

≈ **Mini Lesson:** The word of God is not *as* powerful but *more* powerful than the sword (perhaps this is another reason Captain Moroni bore his testimony to Zerahemnah and his armies). All of mankind's efforts to bring peace to the world will fail without God. The world will only change when hearts are changed. President Boyd K. Packer taught, "True doctrine, understood, changes attitudes and behavior. The study of the doctrines of the gospel will improve behavior quicker than a study of behavior will improve behavior" ("Little Children," *Ensign,* November 1986, 17). ≈

That is why we do missionary work. That is why we hold family home evening. That is why we go to seminary and

Sunday School. Because we want to get young people into the Church? No. Because we want the Church to get into young people. When the gospel is in your heart, you are armed, prepared, and fortified. When the word of God gets inside, it is "more powerful than the sword," enabling you to handle any attack the world throws at you.

The war chapters, along with the rest of the Book of Mormon, teach the power and importance of the gospel of Jesus Christ. What the world needs now, and what the world needed then, was the word of God—not just in their luggage but also in their heads.

The Family Bible

Old man Higgins built a shelf,
For the family Bible to rest itself,
Lest a sticky finger or a grimy thumb
Might injure the delicate pages some.
He cautioned the children to touch it not,
And it rested there with never a blot,
Though the Higgins tribe is a troublesome lot.

His neighbor, Miggins, built a shelf,
"Come children," he said, "and help yourself."
Now the Miggins Bible is ragged and worn
With some of the choicest pages torn
Where children have fingered and thumbed
    and read,
But of the Miggins children it is said,
Each carries a Bible in his head.
                 (Author unknown)

We live in a nation governed not by a king but by words

(the Constitution), and one day the Lord Jesus Christ will return to earth to reign. Interestingly, one of Jesus' titles is "The Word" (John 1:1–3).

Here We Go Again

Well, at least Zerahemnah was gone, and his armies made a covenant to stay away. The Nephites could now live in relative peace for a time, safe from external threats. It appears that Helaman listened to the prophecies of his father, Alma, and he knew what the children of Lehi would face in the future. More internal dissensions and wars would come. Helaman knew that the people's best defense and preparation was to be deeply rooted in the word of God, so he "went forth to establish the church again in all the land," appointing priests and teachers over all the churches (Alma 45:22).

Sadly, however, it wasn't long until the pride cycle resumed. The Nephites' most dangerous enemy was not outside the city walls but inside the people's hearts. Enjoying the blessings of relative peace and prosperity, some "grew proud, being lifted up in their hearts, because of their exceedingly great riches," and they "would not give heed to [Helaman's] words, to walk uprightly before God" (Alma 45:24). Clearly, Nephite pride was more dangerous than Lamanite aggression.

Bottom line? Their wealth increased, but their spirituality decreased. And within the spiritually disintegrating Nephite society, a new opponent of Captain Moroni emerged—an opponent so treacherous and murderous as to shake the foundations of the Nephite government. The movement this new enemy initiated would result in death and destruction among the Nephites for the next thirteen years.

Lessons from Alma 45

1. The word of God is a stabilizing force in society.
2. The word of God is the first and best preparation for facing a world in turmoil.
3. Pride is more dangerous than aggression.

CHAPTER 4

ALMA 46–47

Don't Come Down
from Your Mountain!

Amalickiah conspires to be king—Moroni raises the title of liberty—He rallies the people to defend their religion—True believers are called Christians—A remnant of Joseph shall be preserved—Amalickiah and the dissenters flee to the land of Nephi—Those who will not support the cause of freedom are put to death. Amalickiah uses treachery, murder, and intrigue to become king of the Lamanites—The Nephite dissenters are more wicked and ferocious than the Lamanites (ALMA 46–47 HEADNOTES).

The story in these chapters has a "major lesson" that is one of my favorites in all of the war chapters. Fasten your seatbelts, readers; we're going in.

Business philosopher Jim Rohn once taught, "If your name ever appears in a book, make sure that it's an example, not a warning" *(The Art of Exceptional Living* [New York: Simon & Schuster, 1994], audiocassette). The name

Amalickiah appears in the Book of Mormon as a warning, and it is forever associated with these chilling verses: "Thus we see how quick the children of men do forget the Lord their God, yea, how quick to do iniquity, and to be led away by the evil one. Yea, and we also see the great wickedness one very wicked man can cause to take place among the children of men" (Alma 46:8–9).

Amalickiah was slick. Just reading about this guy gives me the creeps. He was flattering, cunning, and treacherous, and he didn't mind killing people to get what he wanted. Amalickiah was a Nephite who caused all kinds of problems because of his political ambitions. (As mentioned before, Nephite apostates caused more problems for the Nephites than the Lamanites did.) Amalickiah just couldn't wait to be king, and he had the support of many of the lower judges who, unlike Captain Moroni, were also "seeking for power" (Alma 46:4).

Kings Are a Royal Pain

The Nephites had lived under the inspired system of judges for nineteen years, but now, some of the people wanted a change. Why would they want a change in the government? Was there something wrong with the judge system? No. It promoted freedom and liberty, and it controlled ambition with built-in checks and balances. But governments are only good when the people are good. As founding father John Adams observed, "Our Constitution was made only for a moral and religious people. It is wholly inadequate to the government of any other" (in *America's*

God and Country, comp. William J. Federer [Coppell, Texas: FAME Publishing, 1994], 10–11).

Amalickiah and his followers were not moral or religious, as evidenced by the fact that they "would not hearken to the words of Helaman and his brethren" (Alma 46:1). Having Amalickiah as king of the Nephites would have been disastrous.

> ➥ **Observation:** King Benjamin and King Mosiah were righteous kings, and when Jesus comes again we'll have a righteous king. But both the Book of Mormon and the Old Testament describe the problems of having a king. The ancient Israelites wanted a king, and when Samuel brought their request before the Lord, the Lord responded, "They have not rejected thee, but they have rejected me, that I should not reign over them" (1 Samuel 8:7). Alma the Elder taught, "If it were possible that ye could always have just men to be your kings it would be well for you to have a king" (Mosiah 23:8). Alma, as you recall, served under wicked King Noah and was personally affected and nearly destroyed by his wickedness. The problem is, kings and their successors often become dictators. When the Jaredites arrived in the promised land, they wanted a king too, which caused the brother of Jared to make this prophetic observation: "Surely this thing leadeth into captivity" (Ether 6:23). Surely it did. ◄

That's the problem—what if your king becomes unrighteous? What if he becomes a dictator? How do you kick him out? He probably won't want to leave, so he'll have to be forced out.

Next on Headline News

Removing an unjust king is difficult, to say the least. Notice how much these verses from King Mosiah remind us of world events in the latter days.

> And behold, now I say unto you, ye cannot dethrone an iniquitous king save it be through much contention, and the shedding of much blood. For behold, he has his friends in iniquity, and he keepeth his guards about him; and he teareth up the laws of those who have reigned in righteousness before him; and he trampleth under his feet the commandments of God;
>
> And he enacteth laws, and sendeth them forth among his people, yea, laws after the manner of his own wickedness; and whosoever doth not obey his laws he causeth to be destroyed; and whosoever doth rebel against him he will send his armies against them to war, and if he can he will destroy them; and thus an unrighteous king doth pervert the ways of all righteousness (Mosiah 29:21–23).

Does that remind you of a situation that's been in the news for the past couple of years? Perhaps that's why Hugh Nibley once said, "Wo to the generation that understands the Book of Mormon!" (*An Approach to the Book of Mormon,* in *The Collected Works of Hugh Nibley,* 3d ed., 14 vols. [Salt Lake City and Provo, Utah: Deseret Book and the

Foundation for Ancient Research and Mormon Studies, 1988], 6:119).

Place Reminders of Your Covenants Everywhere

Captain Moroni was well aware of the risks of having a king. Responding to the movement of Amalickiah and his supporters, Moroni "rent his coat; and he took a piece thereof, and wrote upon it—In memory of our God, our religion, and freedom, and our peace, our wives, and our children—and he fastened it upon the end of a pole" and called it "the title of liberty" (Alma 46:12–13).

Moroni understood perfectly the oft-repeated promise of the Book of Mormon that if the children of Lehi kept the commandments they would prosper in the land (1 Nephi 4:14). He knew that if their system crumbled, they would have no one to blame but themselves. Moroni proclaimed, "Surely God shall not suffer that we, who are despised because we take upon us the name of Christ, shall be trodden down and destroyed, until we bring it upon us by our own transgressions" (Alma 46:18).

Captain Moroni went from place to place inviting the people to accept the title of liberty by covenant and to fight if necessary to maintain liberty in their lands. Meanwhile, "Amalickiah saw that the people of Moroni were more numerous than the Amalickiahites" (Alma 46:29). When Amalickiah read the headlines, he said, "We're outta here." He then took his followers and fled into the wilderness. Because Moroni knew that Amalickiah would strengthen the Lamanites, he ordered a pursuit. Unfortunately, Amalickiah escaped, but some of his followers were brought back and given the opportunity to "enter into a covenant to support the cause of freedom" (Alma 46:35). Oddly enough, a few actually refused, preferring to die rather than to maintain a free government—kind of a "Give me bondage or give me death" situation!

Captain Moroni "caused the title of liberty to be hoisted upon every tower" (Alma 46:36). Towers appear to be the modern media of that time, and they reminded the Nephites in all parts of the land of their covenants. Imagine what a different world we would have today if our media *reminded* us of our covenants rather than persuade us to *abandon* them.

> ≈ **Mini Lesson:** We too can place reminders of our covenants everywhere. President Spencer W. Kimball counseled families to display pictures of the temple in their homes to remind youth of their goal to be temple worthy and to remind parents of their temple covenants. The way we dress, the way we talk, the modern media with which we surround ourselves should all be reminders and supporters of our covenants. As someone once said, "Be careful how you act—you may be the only standard work some people will ever read!" ≈

They'll be Coming Down the Mountain When They Come

Amalickiah and his followers escaped into the land of Nephi (where the Lamanites lived) and immediately began to incite the Lamanites to anger against the Nephites, which is exactly what Moroni thought might happen. The king of the Lamanites was easily persuaded and made a proclamation that the armies of the Lamanites should prepare to attack the Nephites.

The larger part of the Lamanite army, however, was afraid of attacking the Nephites and ran away. Amalickiah was given charge of the smaller part of the army that was willing to attack the Nephites and was ordered to compel the rest of the army to fight. Those who didn't want to fight appointed a man named Lehonti to be their leader, and they "gathered themselves together upon the top of the mount which was called Antipas" (Alma 47:7).

Amalickiah sent a secret embassy up the mountain to invite Lehonti to come down and speak with him, but Lehonti refused. Twice more Amalickiah invited Lehonti for a chat, but the people of Lehonti were "fixed in their minds with a determined resolution that they would not be subjected to go against the Nephites" (Alma 47:6). Finally, when Amalickiah was convinced "that he could not get Lehonti to come down off from the mount," he decided that he would go up, "nearly to Lehonti's camp" (Alma 47:12).

Okay, now listen with your spiritual ears. On his fourth try, Amalickiah invited Lehonti to come down "just a little" and to keep his guards with him if he felt unprotected. Lehonti finally agreed. Then, lying through his traitorous teeth, Amalickiah said, "Hey, I'm not really your enemy. I'm your friend." Amalickiah told Lehonti that he didn't want to battle with his reluctant armies. He had a better plan.

Amalickiah suggested that Lehonti bring his army down in the nighttime and surround Amalickiah's army while his men slept. Amalickiah said that when his army awoke and saw themselves surrounded, they would surrender, and the entire Lamanite army would be united again—just one big happy army. In exchange for his surrender, Amalickiah would be appointed "second leader," and Lehonti would take command of the entire force. The plan worked, and Amalickiah became second in command. However, Amalickiah's clever scheme was just getting started. He didn't tell the whole truth to Lehonti—he had only shared the first part of his plan.

Question: How does one who is second in command become first in command?

Answer: He removes the commander.

Oops! Lehonti should never have come down from his mountain. He was in grave danger, and he didn't even know it. The murderous "Amalickiah caused that one of his servants should administer poison by degrees to Lehonti, that he died" (Alma 47:18). Amalickiah pulled it off. He was now first in command of the entire Lamanite army.

But Amalickiah *still* had not completed his evil plans. He marched back to the king of the Lamanites with the entire army, and while the king was welcoming the servants of Amalickiah, one of them "stabbed the king to the heart" (Alma 47:24). Immediately Amalickiah's servants accused the king's own servants of committing the crime. Eventually Amalickiah won over the king's widow and became the king of the Lamanites! Can you believe this?

"And thus by his fraud, and by the assistance of his cunning servants, he obtained the kingdom" (Alma 47:35). Originally he wanted to rule over the Nephites. Now he was ruling over the Lamanites. But he wasn't done yet.

"Is There Not a Type in This Thing?"

Do you know what a scriptural type is? You've probably learned about it in seminary, but if you don't know yet, you will. Here's a quick example: Moses was a type of Christ. Moses led the children of Israel out of bondage, through the waters of the Red Sea, to mount Sinai, and to the promised land. Similarly Jesus led the children of Israel out of bondage (spiritual bondage), through the waters of baptism, to the mountain of the Lord (the temple), and into the celestial kingdom. The scriptures are full of types. In fact, Nephi taught that "all things which have been given of God from the beginning of the world, unto man, are the typifying of [Christ]" (2 Nephi 11:4).

When I first started studying the story of Amalickiah, I wondered if Amalickiah could be considered as a type of Satan. Now I've gone to the other extreme. I think that Amalickiah as a type of Satan is pretty hard to miss. Amalickiah's rise to power and his escape from Nephite society remind us of Satan's power play and expulsion in the premortal life. Satan's continued efforts to enslave and addict the children of God are like Amalickiah's plan to bring the Nephites into bondage. Additionally many of the same words used in the Book of Mormon to describe Satan are also used to describe Amalickiah. Some of the ways in which Amalickiah resembles Satan appear in the chart at right.

Perhaps the most compelling example of Amalickiah's devil-like role involved his subtle but deadly plan to persuade Lehonti to leave his place of safety. Amalickiah, like Satan,

AMALICKIAH AS A TYPE OF SATAN

AMALICKIAH	SATAN
"Desirous to be a king" (Alma 46:4).	"I will exalt my throne above the stars of God" (2 Nephi 24:13).
A Nephite and "the leader of those who were wroth against" Helaman and his brethren (Alma 46:3).	"An angel of God who was in authority in the presence of God, who rebelled against the Only Begotten Son" (D&C 76:25).
Sought "to destroy the church of God, and to destroy the foundation of liberty" (Alma 46:10).	"Sought to destroy the agency of man" (Moses 4:3).
"Fled with a small number of his men" (Alma 46:33).	Was cast out, "and, at that day, many followed after him" (Abraham 3:28).
"A man of many flattering words" (Alma 46:10).	"Others he flattereth away" (2 Nephi 28:22).
"A man of cunning device" (Alma 46:10).	"O that cunning plan of the evil one" (2 Nephi 9:28).
A man who "murdered" the king (Alma 55:5).	"A murderer from the beginning" (John 8:44).
Claimed not to be the enemy but desired to be the "leader and . . . chief commander" over the whole army (Alma 47:19–20).	"I am no devil, for there is none" (2 Nephi 28:22).
"Did care not for the blood of his people" (Alma 49:10).	"The devil will not support his children at the last day" (Alma 30:60).
Poisoned Lehonti carefully, or "by degrees" (Alma 47:18).	"Leadeth them away carefully down to hell" (2 Nephi 28:21).
"Determined . . . to overpower the Nephites and to bring them into bondage" (Alma 48:4).	"Grasps them with his awful chains, from whence there is no deliverance" (2 Nephi 28:22).

says, "Come down from your mountain and just talk to me." Lehonti led his armies to mount Antipas for refuge. Symbolically speaking, mountains are higher ground, often associated with temples and temple covenants. Ancient prophets were often told to go up into the mountains—kind of like meeting God halfway. Today temples are our refuge from the world.

Like Amalickiah, Satan urges us to come down from our mountains, or to leave our covenants. When we refuse Satan's invitations, "being fixed in [our] minds with a determined resolution" (Alma 47:6), he says, "Okay, bring your guards with you, and *just come down a little*." See how subtle he is? It's interesting that Amalickiah invited Lehonti down three times. Similarly, Satan tried to tempt Jesus in three different ways when the Savior was "led up of the Spirit into the wilderness," set "on a pinnacle of the temple," and taken to "an exceeding high mountain"—but Jesus never came down (Matthew 4:1–11).

Brother S. Michael Wilcox commented on Amalickiah's (and Satan's) tactic of bringing his prey to lower ground while deceiving him into thinking that he was still in charge:

> "You're in control! I only want to talk! You have your guards! You only have to come down a little bit!" Amalickiah assures his victim. Lehonti, feeling secure although undoubtedly mistrustful, made his first mistake: He descended from the heights of the mountain. In his own mind, however, he was still safe, because he was in control (*Don't Leap with the Sheep* [Salt Lake City: Deseret Book, 2001], 35–36).

Once you've left your stronghold, Satan pacifies you with half-truths that hide his real intentions. Eventually he persuades you to come all the way down while maintaining the illusion that he's really not an enemy but a friend. Remember, Satan whispers, "I am no devil, for there is none" (2 Nephi 28:22).

When a Little Is a Lot

Eventually Satan's plan for the deceived becomes deadly as he poisons them, not all at once, but "by degrees." What a perfectly descriptive phrase! When Mormon abridged this story, he could have told us simply, "The servant of Amalickiah killed Lehonti," or "the servant of Amalickiah poisoned Lehonti." But Mormon gave us two extra words that speak volumes: Lehonti was poisoned "by degrees."

"By degrees" accurately describes Satan's strategy of incremental entrapment. I like to call it his "lie upon lie, decept upon decept" strategy of leading his captives "carefully down to hell" (2 Nephi 28:21). Giving an inch is still losing ground, and little compromises eventually become large concessions. Here's another scripture that describes how Satan's control grows stronger and stronger "by degrees": he "leadeth them by the neck with a flaxen cord, until he bindeth them with his strong cords forever" (2 Nephi 26:22).

What makes Satan's "by degrees" strategy so cunning is that his victims are often completely unaware that anything bad is happening. Their downfall is much like Lehonti's. He thought he was still in command until the very moment he was murdered.

❦ **Major Lesson:** This one is terribly obvious. *Don't come down from your mountain!* The young women stand up each week and say, "We are daughters of our Heavenly Father, who loves us, and we love Him. We will 'stand as witnesses of God at all times and in all things, and in all places.'" The young men say they will "become converted to the gospel of Jesus Christ and live by its teachings." Satan wants us to come down from our mountain, so he repeatedly invites us to leave higher ground. If we won't come down all the way, he invites us to come down just a little. ❦

Amalickiah was an enemy in disguise. Sometimes those who invite you down are pretending to be friends, but they should give you the creeps. If someone tells you that he's your friend but then asks you to compromise your standards just a little, the story of Amalickiah and Lehonti should come rushing to your mind. Lehonti probably said, "I know what I'm doing," not recognizing that he was being slowly poisoned by someone pretending to be on his side.

Have your parents or leaders ever said to you, "That person may be a bad influence on you"? It's hard to hear that kind of thing, isn't it? We might become a little defensive, and think, "Hey, I know what I'm doing." But do you know what? Your parents or leaders may be right. They may see you gradually changing even though you may not even see it happening. But maybe your clothes or the music you listen to or the movies you watch or the friends you hang out with *are* changing. Be aware that sometimes we can be blinded to something right in front of our noses. The adults in your life may see something you don't even recognize. They may see an Amalickiah trying to poison you "by degrees."

Yikes. Don't ever tell me we can't apply the war chapters to our lives. We can, and we should (and we will).

Well, back to the story. Believe it or not, Amalickiah became king of the Lamanites. He left a few dead people in his path, but he got what he wanted—the throne and the kingdom. Do you think that accomplishment satisfied his ambitions? No way. He was just getting started. In Amalickiah's case, the wicked just get wickeder (or, to put it properly, more wicked). So shields up, Book of Mormon explorers, we're moving on to Alma 48.

Lessons from Alma 46–47

1. Kings lead to bondage.
2. Place reminders of your covenants everywhere.
3. Don't come down from your mountain. "Stand ye in holy places, and be not moved" (D&C 87:8).
4. Beware of "little" temptations that trick you into thinking, "I'm still in control."
5. Beware of "friends" who tempt you.

CHAPTER 5

ALMA 48

Make Covenants, Then Make Swords

Amalickiah incites the Lamanites against the Nephites—Moroni prepares his people to defend the cause of the Christians—He rejoiced in liberty and freedom and was a mighty man of God (ALMA 48 HEADNOTE).

This chapter is short, but its message is terrific. Back in Alma 46 we learned that Amalickiah wanted to be the leader of the Nephites, but now that we're in Alma 48 his real intentions toward his own people are revealed: "As soon as Amalickiah had obtained the kingdom he began to inspire the hearts of the Lamanites against the people of Nephi; yea, he did appoint men to speak unto the Lamanites from their towers, against the Nephites. . . . For he was determined . . . to overpower the Nephites and to bring them into bondage" (Alma 48:1, 4). Aha! Kings really do lead to bondage, and that's what this character wanted all along—to put the Nephites in bondage!

Notice the mass media in these two countries. Their messages are totally different. Moroni has the title of liberty on his towers, while Amalickiah is stirring up anger on his towers. Moroni's towers say, "Love God." Amalickiah's towers say, "Hate Nephites!" (The more I read the Book of Mormon, the more I appreciate the prophet Mormon as an editor and abridger. Mormon continually offers interesting contrasts.)

Faith before Forts

While Amalickiah was deceiving and murdering and poisoning, Moroni was doing something else: "Now it came to pass that while Amalickiah had thus been obtaining power by fraud and deceit, Moroni, on the other hand, had been preparing . . ." (Sorry to stop you in mid-scripture, but what do you think it's going to say? What was Moroni preparing? Forts? Swords? Lehonti Memorial Poison Control Centers? No.) "Moroni, on the other hand, had been preparing *the minds of the people to be faithful unto the Lord their God*" (Alma 48:7; emphasis added).

One lived by fraud and deceit, the other by faith and devotion. Faith in Christ helped the Nephites conquer Zerahemnah, and faith in Christ would help them conquer Amalickiah as well. Interesting, isn't it? Moroni's first priority was not forts and swords but arming his people with righteousness. Once they got their spiritual act together, they could concentrate on lesser priorities, like national defense.

≈ **Mini Lesson**: In war or in peace, the message is clear. Spiritual preparation should always come first.

Get your life in order. Cleanse the inner vessel. Then prepare for the attacks, spiritual and otherwise, which will come. Jesus taught the same thing in the Sermon on the Mount, and the sermon at the temple: "Seek ye first the kingdom of God, and his righteousness; and all these things shall be added unto you" (Matthew 6:33; 3 Nephi 13:33). Our first priority is our own spiritual well-being. ≈

The happiest teenagers I know have their spiritual lives in order. They may lose student elections, they may fail at tryouts, and they may not get asked out on many dates, but they are happy. Despite their trials, they remain cheerful and hopeful. How do they do that? Well, as Elder M. Russell Ballard wrote:

> The best thing about living a Christ-centered life, however, is how it makes you feel—inside. It's hard to have a negative attitude about things if and when your life is focused on the Prince of Peace. There will still be problems. Everyone has them. But faith in the Lord Jesus Christ is a power to be reckoned with in the universe and in individual lives (*Our Search for Happiness: An Invitation to Understand The Church of Jesus Christ of Latter-day Saints* [Salt Lake City: Deseret Book, 1993], 15).

Sometimes deacons and beehives ask me for my autograph. Personally, I feel that my autograph is worth exactly nothing, but some young people still ask for it. So, along with writing my name, I usually add one of my favorite phrases: "Keep the faith." I don't write, "Keep trying to be popular," or "Keep trying to be fashionable." Keeping your spiritual life in order is your first priority because it will keep you on track.

Remember Who You Are and Whom You're Named After

Much of the remainder of chapter 48 is a tribute to Captain Moroni. I know young people whose favorite verse in the Book of Mormon is Alma 48:17:

> Yea, verily, verily I say unto you, if all men had been, and were, and ever would be, like unto Moroni, behold, the very powers of hell would have been shaken forever; yea, the devil would never have power over the hearts of the children of men.

Clearly the prophet Mormon, who lived more than four hundred years after these events, loved, admired, and rejoiced in the greatness of Captain Moroni. Perhaps that is why Mormon named his own son Moroni. Whenever I drive by a temple and see Moroni sounding his trumpet, I think of both of these men—Captain Moroni and Moroni the son of Mormon. Their lives, their teachings, and their examples gave honor to the name they shared.

The war chapters validate the promise of the Book of Mormon. If the children of Lehi would keep the commandments, they would prosper in the land. Notice how Helaman and his brethren kept the Nephites free from internal strife for the next four years:

> And the people did humble themselves *because of*

their words, insomuch that they were highly favored of the Lord, and thus they were free from wars and contentions among themselves, yea, even for the space of four years (Alma 48:20; emphasis added).

Though the Nephites' internal problems ceased for a time, Amalickiah and the Lamanites continued to pose an external threat.

A Sorry State of Affairs

For the Nephites, there would be more battles, more death, and more war. But the war chapters teach us the attitude that disciples of Christ should have in time of war.

> Their wars never did cease for the space of many years with the Lamanites, notwithstanding their much reluctance. Now, they were sorry to take up arms against the Lamanites, because they did not delight in the shedding of blood; yea, and this was not all—they were sorry to be the means of sending so many of their brethren out of this world into an eternal world, unprepared to meet their God (Alma 48:22–23).

The righteous Nephites were reluctant warriors, and because of their reluctance, sorrow, and defensive posture, they qualified as righteous warriors. They did not want to spend their lives fighting, as the record repeatedly suggests. They were not warmongers looking for a fight. But they could not allow their families to be massacred or placed into bondage.

Lessons from Alma 48

1. Spiritual preparation is our first priority. Temporal preparation is also important, but we must get our spiritual lives in order first.
2. The Christian's attitude toward war should be sorrow and reluctance.

CHAPTER 6

ALMA 49

If Ye Are Prepared
Ye Shall Not Fear

*The invading Lamanites are unable to take the fortified cities
of Ammonihah and Noah—Amalickiah curses God and swears
to drink the blood of Moroni—Helaman and his brethren continue to strengthen the Church* (ALMA 49 HEADNOTE).

This is another short chapter, but its message is awesome.
I like to call Alma 49 the "Boy Scout chapter" because it fre-
quently repeats the word *prepared*. "Be prepared" is the offi-
cial motto of the Boy Scouts, and it might have been the
motto of the Nephites as they readied their cities for a
Lamanite invasion.

Back in Alma 43–44 we learned that the Lamanite armies
under Zerahemnah wore only loincloths. At this point, however, the Lamanites wised up a little and showed up wearing
armor. But when they came to invade they were confronted
with something else they didn't expect—the Nephites had
armored their *cities,* and the Lamanites were absolutely

amazed at what they saw. In fact, they were astonished—something the people always seem to be in the Book of Mormon: "The chief captains of the Lamanites were astonished exceedingly, because of the wisdom of the Nephites in *preparing* their places of security" (Alma 49:5; emphasis added).

Apparently, it wasn't just their preparation but their *manner* of preparation that came from an inspired source. The Nephites were prepared for the Lamanites "in a manner which never had been known among the children of Lehi. Now they were *prepared* for the Lamanites, to battle after the manner of the instructions of Moroni" (Alma 49:8; emphasis added). Aha! Moroni taught them how to prepare.

Remember that the Amalickiahites only recently had been kicked out of Nephite society. You'd think they might have been familiar with how the Nephites would defend their cities, but even they were not acquainted with the nature of Moroni's defenses. "The Lamanites, or the Amalickiahites, were exceedingly astonished at their *manner* of preparation for war" (Alma 49:9; emphasis added).

The World's Way or the Lord's Way?

The spiritual lesson is obvious. Not only will prophets seek to prepare us, but they will also prepare us in an unconventional manner, a manner with which the world is not familiar.

≈ **Mini Lesson:** The Nephites were prepared because they followed the instructions of Moroni. Similarly our best defense is to prepare for our spiritual battles by following the instructions of our inspired leaders no matter how unconventional or unpopular they may seem. One of my favorite quotes from President Ezra Taft Benson compares the way the Lord works with how the world works. "The Lord works from the inside out. The world works from the outside in. The world would take people out of the slums. Christ takes the slums out of people, and then they take themselves out of the slums. The world would mold men by changing their environment. Christ changes men, who then change their environment. The world would shape human behavior, but Christ can change human nature" ("Born of God," *Ensign,* November 1985, 6). ≈

Just think of the difference between what you hear on television and what you hear in seminary. The world says there's nothing wrong with immorality as long as you practice "safe sex." The gospel says, "When the world says 'safe sex,' what that usually means is 'safe immorality,' and there's no such thing." The world says, "The way to be happy is to do whatever you want." The gospel reminds us that "wickedness never was happiness" (Alma 41:10) and that no one has ever said, "I'm a happier person because I broke the law of chastity." The world says, "Wear a sleazy prom dress—look like a pop-star in a music video." The gospel says, "Real beauty is found in modesty," or, as I heard one teenage boy say, "The modest are the hottest." When the world says, "Do what you want," the gospel answers, "Do what you should."

So the Nephites prepared their cities in ingenious ways,

and the Lamanites were so dumbstruck by the inspired defenses of the Nephite city of Ammonihah that they decided, "Gee, we'd better find a weaker city to attack."

"Fight Really Hard, Boys, and All This Will Be *Mine!*"

The Book of Mormon tells us that Amalickiah wasn't leading his forces into battle at this point. He stayed safely at home in the land of Nephi. This was actually a good thing for the Lamanite armies because Mormon tells us that if Amalickiah had led the invasion, he would have attacked Ammonihah anyway. "For behold, he did care not for the blood of his people" (Alma 49:10). Amalickiah was more concerned about gaining his objectives than losing his armies.

➡ **Observation:** Amalickiah's "I don't care how many have to die" attitude toward his own armies reminds me of something. In the closing scenes of the Book of Mormon, after the Nephites are destroyed, Moroni (the son of Mormon) reports that "the Lamanites are at war one with another; and the whole face of this land is one continual round of murder and bloodshed; and no one knoweth the end of the war" (Mormon 8:8). Once the Lamanites finished off the Nephites, they turned on each other. Apparently, Satan's goal was not limited to simply destroying the Nephites. Once he accomplished that goal, he inspired the Lamanites to fight among themselves. Like Amalickiah, Satan does not support those who do his dirty work. His goal is to send people, *any* people—Nephites, Lamanites, or any manner of "ites"—out of this world "unprepared to meet their God" (Alma 48:23). Captain Moroni, by contrast, cared deeply for people, including the Lamanites. He wanted all people to repent, and he rejoiced when he could accomplish his objectives without shedding blood. ◄

Back to the story. After abandoning their designs to attack the city of Ammonihah, the Lamanites marched toward the city of Noah and were once again—what's my favorite word?—astonished! "To their astonishment, the city of Noah, which had hitherto been a weak place, had now, by the means of Moroni, become strong, yea, even to exceed the strength of the city Ammonihah" (Alma 49:14).

Did you notice that? By the means of *Moroni,* something that was *weak* became *strong.* What scripture does that remind you of? Yup, Ether 12:27. If we come unto *Christ,* he will make our *weak* things *strong.* (I liked this connection so much that I wrote Ether 12:27 in the margin of my scriptures. You might want to do so as well.)

When Amalickiah received word of his army's failed objectives, he threw a fit!

> He did curse God, and also Moroni, swearing with an oath that he would drink his blood; and this because Moroni had kept the commandments of God in preparing for the safety of his people. And it came to pass, that on the other hand, the people of Nephi did thank the Lord their God, because of his

matchless power in delivering them from the hands of their enemies (Alma 49:27–28).

Wow, isn't that an interesting contrast? One *curses* God and swears a murderous oath, while others *thank* God for deliverance from their enemies.

The Power of the Word

How do the Nephites account for their success? Superior tactics? Fortified cities? Inspired generals? They had all of those, but that's not where they give credit:

> Yea, and there was continual peace among them, and exceedingly great prosperity in the church *because of their heed and diligence which they gave unto the word of God,* which was declared unto them by Helaman, and Shiblon, and Corianton, and Ammon and his brethren, yea, and by all those who had been ordained by the holy order of God, being baptized unto repentance, and sent forth to preach among the people (Alma 49:30; emphasis added).

Okay, seminary scholars, help me out here by filling in the blanks below. (Hint: Ephesians 6:14–17.) If we're wearing the "whole armor of God," that means we have:

Our loins girt about with T _____
The breastplate of R _____
Our feet shod with the preparation of the gospel of
    P _____
The shield of F _____
The helmet of S _____

Now, picture all of us wearing the armor listed above, and you'll notice something. We're totally defensive. We have no weapon! We've got armor but nothing to fight back with, and we're going to get totally beat up, right? Wrong. I left out something. The last thing:

The sword of the S _____
Which is the W _____ ___ _____

Very interesting. To physically defend ourselves we need a sword. And to spiritually defend ourselves we need a sword too. Swords of steel did not give the Nephites victory, but obedience to "the sword of the Spirit, which is the word of God" did (Ephesians 6:17). The Nephites listened to Moroni, and they armed themselves with the word of God taught by Helaman and others. That was their sword, and it's our sword too.

Lessons from Alma 49

1. Be prepared! Total reliance on God does not mean total inaction on our part.
2. Prophets prepare us in unconventional ways. The Lord's ways are not the world's ways.
3. The sword of the Spirit, which is the word of God, is our weapon to see us through our spiritual battles.

CHAPTER 7

ALMA 50

Fortifications and
Watchmen on the Towers

Moroni fortifies the lands of the Nephites—They build many new cities—Wars and destructions befell the Nephites in the days of their wickedness and abominations—Morianton and his dissenters are defeated by Teancum—Nephihah dies and his son Pahoran fills the judgment-seat (ALMA 50 HEADNOTE).

When You're Through Preparing, You're Through

Despite all of the preparations the Nephites had made in Alma 49, Alma 50 begins by telling us "that Moroni did not stop making preparations" (Alma 50:1). First, he ordered the cities to be encircled by heaps of earth. That would likely take a while. If I had to encircle just my house with dirt, I would wear out a few shovels, and the resulting blisters would consume an entire box of bandages. So you can only imagine the incredible amount of work and blisters involved in encircling an entire city!

Do you think the workers might have complained? "Um, Moroni, I have homework." You can imagine Moroni responding, "Hmmm, we're not done yet. Let's place works of timbers up to the height of a man on top of the heaps."

Wow! When was the last time you built a work of timbers to the height of a man? Yeah, it's been a long time for me too. Perhaps the workers were looking for a way out. "But Moroni, we were going to hang out with friends tonight."

Moroni still wasn't finished. "Let's make a frame of pickets atop the work of timbers. Make it strong and high." The workers must have been exhausted by the time they finished.

"Okay, Captain, we've done enough already. We think this will keep them out."

But Moroni knew they needed more. "No, we need a couple of more things—let's build towers above the pickets, and let's put people in the towers." It would have been easy for the workers to say, "Moroni, were tired. Can we go home and take a nap?"

Spiritual Fortification

Perhaps there's a lesson within these levels of defense. It wasn't just heaps of earth but heaps of earth capped with works of timbers that surrounded the cities. And it wasn't just heaps and timbers but heaps, timbers, pickets, and towers that created places of security. All of these things worked together to provide a formidable barrier to the enemy.

≈ **Mini Lesson:** My friend and institute teacher Todd Murdock suggested that all these defenses could be compared to the "little things" we've been asked to do to fortify our spirits:

Heaps are like prayer: "Um, Mom, I have homework."

Timbers are like family home evening: "But Mom, I was going to hang out with my friends tonight."

Pickets are like personal scripture study: "Mom, I've done enough already."

Towers are like service to others: "Mom, I'm tired. Can I go take a nap?"

Personal and family prayer are great, but we need more protection. Daily prayer with scripture study is better. Daily prayer with scripture study *and* service to others is better still. When we *know* what to do and *do* what we *know*, we start to become something different. Then we gain internal spiritual defenses against temptation.

Elder M. Russell Ballard taught, "There is not one great and grand thing we can do to arm ourselves spiritually. True spiritual power lies in numerous smaller acts woven together in a fabric of spiritual fortification" ("'Be Strong in the Lord, and in the Power of his Might,'" *Brigham Young University 2001–2002 Speeches* [Provo, Utah: Brigham Young University Publications & Graphics, 2002], 223). ≈

If I had to choose my favorite from among the heaps, pickets, timbers, and towers, I would definitely pick the towers. Actually it's not the towers that protected the Nephites but the watchmen *on* the towers—watchmen who could see the enemy coming from far away.

A Seer is a See-er

Notice how the Lord called Ezekiel to be a prophet: "Son of man, I have made thee a watchman unto the house of Israel: therefore hear the word at my mouth, and give them warning from me" (Ezekiel 3:17). Watchmen are like the eyes on the threat board—the warning system for protection from the enemy.

Every six months we are privileged to sustain prophets, seers, and revelators in general conference. Brother S. Michael Wilcox has written:

> The word *seer* is better understood if we spell it fully—*see-er*. A seer is one who sees. The word *revelator* is associated with *seer*. A revelator is one who reveals. What does he reveal? He reveals what he sees. For this reason the prophets, seers, and revelators of the Church are called by the scriptures the "watchman upon the tower" *(Don't Leap with the Sheep* [Salt Lake City: Deseret Book, 2001], 58).

In another scripture the Lord explained the purpose of the watchmen upon the towers: "Behold, the watchman upon the tower would have seen the enemy while he was yet afar off; and then ye could have made ready and kept the enemy from breaking down the hedge thereof, and saved my vineyard from the hands of the destroyer" (D&C 101:54).

Now let's imagine that we're down below among the heaps, timbers, and pickets. Can we see the enemy coming? No. Our vision is blocked by heaps, timbers, pickets, and towers. We can only see the situation right around us. But imagine the perspective available to a watchman! Towering above the city, he has a 360-degree view of the horizon. Those in the towers, after all, are entrusted with protecting the entire city!

≈ **Mini Lesson:** Can you imagine the watchman warning those below of incoming danger? Can you see how stupid it would be to look up to the watchman and say, "Well, I think you're out of touch," or "Those things don't affect me," or "I don't see what's wrong with that." Or, to put it in *For the Strength of Youth* terms:

Warning—Don't get tattoos and body piercings: "Well, I think you're out of touch."

Warning—Don't see vulgar, immoral, violent, or pornographic entertainment: "Those things don't affect me."

Warning—Don't dress immodestly: "I don't see what's wrong with that."

If we don't see what's wrong with the enemy's threats, perhaps it's because we don't *see*. *Seers see.* Our very lives may depend on obeying the words of the watchmen. Those of us who serve below must be humble enough to realize that the watchman can see things we cannot. Ignoring the watchman would be just about the dumbest thing we could do. It would be like having no watchman at all. Or, as Sheri Dew has written, "If we don't listen to the prophet, we might as well not have one" (*No Doubt about It* [Salt Lake City, Bookcraft, 2001], 174). ≋

So Alma 50 teaches us that we fortify ourselves physically *and* spiritually. Without the heaps, timbers, pickets, towers, and watchmen, the Nephites would have been in "heap" big trouble.

Rest Assured

Having a leader like Moroni must have given the people some confidence. In fact, Alma 50:12 says that Moroni's armies increased "because of the *assurance of protection* which his works did bring forth unto them" (Alma 50:12, emphasis added). Moroni and his armies worked! They didn't sit around singing "Kumbaya," "Que Sera Sera," or "Hakuna Matata." They did everything in their power to fortify their cities, and they placed their faith in the Lord to protect them from their enemies.

When you do your part and ask the Lord to do his part, you begin to feel assured. Paul wrote, "Faith is the *assurance* of things hoped for, the evidence of things not seen" (JST, Hebrews 11:1; emphasis added). Similarly our individual faith in Christ becomes an "assurance of protection." The prophet Joseph Smith wrote from Liberty Jail, "Therefore, dearly beloved brethren, let us cheerfully do all things that lie in our power; and then may we stand still, with the *utmost assurance,* to see the salvation of God, and for his arm to be revealed" (D&C 123:17; emphasis added).

"Thus We See," or "Listen Up"

Every once in a while the Book of Mormon says, "Thus we see." This is the prophet Mormon saying, "Hey, here's the reason I included this, so pay attention." Alma 50 shows that Moroni's work resulted in a period of prosperity for the Nephites, causing Mormon to insert one of his important "thus we see" statements:

> And thus we see how merciful and just are all the dealings of the Lord, to the fulfilling of all his words unto the children of men; yea, we can behold that his words are verified, even at this time, which he spake unto Lehi, saying: Blessed art thou and thy children; and they shall be blessed, inasmuch as they shall keep my commandments they shall prosper in the land. But remember, inasmuch as they will not keep my commandments they shall be cut off from the presence of the Lord.
>
> And we see that these promises have been verified to the people of Nephi; for it has been their quarrelings and their contentions, yea, their murderings, and their plunderings, their idolatry, their whoredoms, and their abominations, which were among themselves, which brought upon them their wars and their destructions.
>
> And those who were faithful in keeping the commandments of the Lord were delivered at all times,

whilst thousands of their wicked brethren have been consigned to bondage, or to perish by the sword, or to dwindle in unbelief, and mingle with the Lamanites (Alma 50:19–22).

Well, the Nephites lived in peace for a time, except for a small border dispute involving a man named Morianton that was quickly put down by one of Moroni's commanders named Teancum. Later, Pahoran was appointed to fill the judgment seat in the stead of his father, Nephihah.

A Chief Judge's Chief Duties

What are governments for anyway? Good question. If you pay attention in civics class or listen to talk radio, you might notice that what governments do, or what people *think* they should do, is a continual debate. Alma 50:39 provides us with an interesting list of at least some of the roles of the ancient Nephite government by stating that Pahoran took the judgment seat with an "oath and sacred ordinance" to:

- Judge righteously.
- Keep the peace and the freedom of the people.
- Grant unto the people their sacred privileges to worship the Lord their God.
- Support and maintain the cause of God all his days.
- Bring the wicked to justice according to their crimes.

Within that verse, we notice things like a judicial system and a penal system, law enforcement and national defense, and freedom of conscience and worship. Under the system of judges, which was a good system, people were governed by law, not by other men. But hang on to your hat because Alma 51 is coming, and there are still a few Nephites out there who would prefer to have a king. They're going to make another attempt to remove the chief judge and set up a monarchy.

Lessons from Alma 50

1. Spiritual fortification comes from doing many things.
2. Watchmen on the towers see things we cannot.
3. Faith and works bring assurance.

CHAPTER 8

ALMA 51

Pride: Thinking You're Strong Makes You Weak

The king-men seek to change the law and set up a king—Pahoran and the freemen are supported by the voice of the people—Moroni compels the king-men to defend their liberty or be put to death—Amalickiah and the Lamanites capture many fortified cities—Teancum repels the Lamanite invasion and slays Amalickiah in his tent (ALMA 51 HEADNOTE).

Oh boy, here we go again. When readers of the Book of Mormon see the word *prosperity* they know what's coming—another whirlwind tour through the Book of Mormon pride cycle. In the twenty-first year of the reign of the judges, the people began to "prosper exceedingly" (Alma 50:18), and now, four years later, another group (or perhaps remnants of an earlier group) emerged that wanted to abolish the system of judges and install a king.

Who in the world would want to do that? The king-men, that's who, or, as Hugh Nibley calls them, the "royalists."

Mormon tells us, "Now those who were in favor of kings were those of high birth, and they sought to be kings; and they were supported by those who sought power and authority over the people" (Alma 51:8). For some reason these people of "high birth" thought they deserved to be in charge of others. Their desire was all about pride and power. By contrast Moroni wrote, "I seek not for power, but to pull it down" (Alma 60:36).

The Nephites finally put the whole thing to a vote, and "the voice of the people" (Alma 51:7) reaffirmed the desire of the populace to maintain a system of judges with Pahoran as chief judge. It sounds as if the people remembered the title of liberty and the fact that kings often lead to bondage.

Meanwhile, back in the land of Nephi, wicked Amalickiah had been at work. He and his armies had been defeated at the cities of Ammonihah and Noah (back in Alma 49), but they had been regrouping, and Amalickiah was gathering a large army to come against the Nephites. When the sore-losing king-men learned that Amalickiah was coming down to battle, "they were glad in their hearts; and they refused to take up arms" (Alma 51:13).

What do you do when a significant part of the population refuses to defend your country? Well, you could take the law into your own hands, but Moroni wasn't like that. He was angry, but he wasn't out of control. Mormon reports that Captain Moroni was "exceedingly wroth because of the stubbornness of those people whom he had labored with so much diligence to preserve" (Alma 51:14). With the backing of the people, Moroni sent a petition that asked the chief judge, Pahoran, for permission to "compel these dissenters to defend their country or to put them to death" (Alma 51:15).

Defending Defense

When I was eighteen, I had to register for the draft. What should be the attitude of Latter-day Saints toward defending their country? Approximately four months after the attack on Pearl Harbor in 1941, President J. Reuben Clark Jr. delivered a message to the Church from the First Presidency. After enumerating many principles from the Doctrine and Covenants, including the sacred nature of the Constitution of the United States, President Clark declared:

> When, therefore, constitutional law, obedient to these principles, calls the manhood of the Church into the armed service of any country to which they owe allegiance, their highest civic duty requires that they meet that call (Conference Report, April 1942, 94).

The people in Moroni's time made their voices heard and decided that all citizens must defend their country. So Moroni, acting legally and following Pahoran's approval of the people's petition, commanded his armies to put down the rebellious king-men.

Weak on the Inside Means Weak on the Outside

While the Nephites were preoccupied with problems on the home front, the Lamanites entered the land of Moroni and took "possession of many cities" (Alma 51:26). Had the

Nephites not faced so many problems at home, Moroni could have positioned his forces to resist the Lamanite invasion.

≈ **Mini Lesson:** Once again we learn that the greatest dangers to the people of God are not external but internal. President Heber J. Grant assured: "Our enemies have never done anything that has injured this work of God, and they never will. I look around, I read, I reflect, and I ask the question, Where are the men of influence, of power and prestige, who have worked against the Latter-day Saints?. . . They have faded away like dew before the sun. We need have no fears, we Latter-day Saints. God will continue to sustain this work; He will sustain the right. If we are loyal, if we are true, if we are worthy of this Gospel, of which God has given us a testimony, there is no danger that the world can ever injure us. We can never be injured, my brethren and sisters, by any mortals, except ourselves. If we fail to serve God, if we fail to do right, then we rob ourselves of the ability and power to grow, to increase in faith and knowledge, to have power with God, and with the righteous (Conference Report, April 1909, 110). ≈

Because of the Nephites' internal problems, the Lamanites occupied many of the cities that Moroni had worked so hard to fortify, "all of which afforded strongholds for the Lamanites" (Alma 51:27). As the Doctrine and Covenants says, if we are not one, we are not the Lord's

(D&C 38:27). And if we are not the Lord's, we are not protected by his power.

Sharp Objects in Tents Can Be Very Intense

After taking many Nephite cities, Amalickiah and his men clashed with the Nephite commander Teancum and his "great warriors." Their battle raged on until dark, when both armies stopped fighting and pitched their tents. But during the night, after Teancum and his servant had crept into the enemy camp, "Teancum stole privily into the tent of the king [Amalickiah], and put a javelin to his heart; and he did cause the death of the king immediately that he did not awake his servants" (Alma 51:31, 34).

As a young man I always admired Teancum. I still do. I admire his courage in sneaking into the camp of the Lamanites, locating the tent of their leader, and sending him to his third estate.

Perhaps Amalickiah and Teancum had once known one another before Amalickiah's pride and ambition got the best of him. Who knows? The important thing was that Amalickiah was gone. Teancum took him out. He didn't poison him "by degrees." He used a more direct approach. He bought him a one-way ticket to the spirit world. Amalickiah was an apostate, a murderer, and a deceiver who did not care for the blood of his own people. His evil ambitions resulted in the death of countless Lamanites and Nephites. There was no room for tolerance or negotiation when it came to Amalickiah. He was evil and hardened, and he had proven it.

When I think of Teancum sending Amalickiah to the

next life with no discussion or debate, I'm reminded of a statement by President Marion G. Romney:

> As a prelude to peace, then, the influence of Satan must be completely subjugated. Even in heaven there could be no peace with him after his rebellion. There, in the world of spirits, the Father and the Son could find no ground upon which they could cooperate with him. He had to be cast out—not compromised with, but cast out ("The Price of Peace," *Ensign*, October 1983, 4–5).

The armies of the Lamanites awakened to find their leader dead. Unfortunately, Amalickiah had a brother named Ammoron who was equally wicked and ambitious. Ammoron became the newest enemy of Captain Moroni, commanding the Lamanites through the remainder of the war chapters.

So the Nephites had a new enemy and a new problem. How could they retake highly fortified cities? We're about to find out in Alma 52.

Lessons from Alma 51

1. People of God have a duty to defend their country.
2. United we stand, divided we fall.

CHAPTER 9

ALMA 52
Don't Leave Your Stronghold!

Ammoron succeeds Amalickiah as king of the Lamanites—
Moroni, Teancum, and Lehi lead the Nephites in a victorious
war against the Lamanites—The city of Mulek is retaken, and
Jacob the Lamanite is slain. (ALMA 52 HEADNOTE).

The Nephite defenses around the perimeter of the land were minimal because their forces were busy at home trying to solve internal problems caused by the king-men. Thus the Lamanites had moved into Nephite lands like a plastic knife through green Jell-O. But when the Lamanites discovered Amalickiah dead in his tent, they immediately discontinued their invasion and took cover in the cities they had already taken from the Nephites. What a rotten situation for the Nephites! The Lamanites were now barricaded inside the cities the Nephites had worked so hard to fortify! How in the world could the Nephites get their cities back?

We Have a Problem—Let's Hold a Meeting

Teancum received orders to retake the city of Mulek but determined that it would be impossible to defeat the Lamanites while they were in their fortifications. When Moroni and his army arrived, the chief captains decided to hold a meeting, or what the Book of Mormon calls a "council of war." First on the agenda was the question of how the Nephites could "flatter [the Lamanites] out of their strongholds" (Alma 52:19).

First they tried Plan A: The Nephites sent embassies to Jacob, the Zoramite leader of the Lamanites, inviting him to bring his armies out of the city of Mulek and meet the Nephites on the plains. Basically what they were requesting was, "Leave your stronghold and come out and fight." Jacob flatly refused. I don't blame him.

So the Nephites tried Plan B. "Moroni, having no hopes of meeting them upon fair grounds, therefore, he resolved upon a plan that he might decoy the Lamanites out of their strongholds." Plan B was a decoy. A decoy is a trick, something that appears to be one thing but is really another. Plan B was ingenious. Moroni's armies marched west of the city of Mulek at night, while Teancum and a few of his men served as the decoy. With Moroni and his men hidden in the wilderness near the city, Teancum and a small number of men marched "down near the seashore," within view of the Lamanites (Alma 52:21, 22).

When the Lamanites saw Teancum and his men, they thought, "Hey, that's a small number. We can take them and be right back!" The decoy worked! Teancum and his men successfully lured, or decoyed, the Lamanite army right out of its fortified city and onto "fair grounds." When Teancum saw the Lamanites coming after him, he maintained the illusion by retreating northward. The Lamanites "took courage and pursued them with vigor" almost all the way to the city of Bountiful (Alma 52:23–24, 27).

I've often wondered if the men in the Nephite armies were enjoying this just a little. I wonder if, when they started running away from the Lamanites, they whispered to each other, "All right, it's working!" I've also wondered if they yelled loudly enough for the Lamanites to overhear, "Oh no, I hope they don't get us!"

The decoy created by Teancum and his men lured the Lamanites farther away from their stronghold than they initially intended to go. And what did the Lamanites encounter when they approached Bountiful? They saw another Nephite army, with Lehi in command, armed, fresh, and full of strength. You can almost see Lehi standing there waving as if to say, "Hi there. We've been waiting for you. You've been stratagemed!"

At the sight of Lehi and his armies, the Lamanites "fled in much confusion," afraid that Lehi might overtake them before they could return to Mulek, the city they had foolishly left. When they turned around in hopes of running back to Mulek, they were shocked to see Captain Moroni and his army behind them, perhaps taunting, "Yoo-hoo, we've been waiting for you too." Surrounded by Lehi on the north and Moroni on the south, Jacob the Zoramite "led the Lamanites forth to battle with exceeding fury against Moroni." Ultimately, many were killed on both sides, but the Nephites gained the upper hand. Moroni then called a cease-fire and offered his enemies benevolent terms of surrender (Alma 52:28, 33, 37).

Oh, Now I Get It!

I must have read this chapter a dozen times looking for a gospel principle or spiritual message. I just about gave up. In fact, on a previous outline I actually wrote, "Maybe just skip Alma 52." I loved the decoy story (and I thought the tactics were interesting), but I didn't know what to learn from it. "There's got to be something in here," I thought, remembering that Nephi had commanded his posterity that "they shall not occupy these plates with things which are not of worth unto the children of men" (1 Nephi 6:6). "Well," I said to myself, "I'm one of the children of men, so what's in here that could be worth something to me?"

Finally I read Alma 52 one more time, and when I closed the book I said to myself, "That's so dumb. Why did the Lamanites leave their stronghold?" Suddenly the lightbulb above my head came on. "Yeah," I repeated to myself, "why did they leave their stronghold?" Why would anyone leave their stronghold? That's such a dumb thing to do! It's bad military strategy, and it's bad spiritual strategy.

Let's review the facts. First the Nephites said, "Come out and meet us on fair grounds." The Lamanites said, "No." Satan doesn't work that openly. He doesn't say, "Come out here so I can tempt you to break the law of chastity." It's just the opposite. Satan doesn't play fair, and he never has. He uses decoys, traps, snares, deceptions, and distractions. He says, "I am no devil, for there is none" (2 Nephi 28:22).

He presents small temptations that might not look like temptations at all. He introduces decoys that lead his victims away "by degrees."

Remember, Teancum was ordered to take "a small number of men" so that they would appear weak and easy to overcome. Remember also that Teancum's group marched away from—not toward—the Lamanite stronghold—another part of the decoy that made them appear to be no threat. Only when the Lamanites *thought* they had an unfair advantage did they venture forth. When we leave or reject our strongholds—our families, our gospel teachings, our true friends—we give Satan an advantage he is happy to exploit.

> ≈ **Major Lesson:** Don't leave your strongholds! In other words, "Stand ye in holy places, and be not moved" (D&C 87:8), or, to echo the Primary song, "Keep the commandments! In this there is safety; in this there is peace" ("Keep the Commandments," *Children's Songbook* [Salt Lake City: The Church of Jesus Christ of Latter-day Saints, 1989], no. 146). It's a simple concept. Simple to understand but hard to follow. It's easy to be flattered or enticed out of the place where we're strongest. Sometimes temptations may seem small or no threat to our spirituality, but they may actually be decoys to lure us away from safety. ≈

Some of you may be thinking, "Wait a sec, Brother Bytheway. Something about your analogy bugs me. Are you comparing the Nephite armies to Satan?" No, I'm not comparing the Nephites to Satan. I am, however, suggesting that *the stratagems of war* are similar to the *stratagems of Satan.*

Stratagems are a common thing in war. Wicked generals and righteous generals have always used them. For example, in the Old Testament we learn how righteous Gideon made an army of three hundred appear to be an army of thousands (Judges 7). At the beginning of the Book of Mormon, we learn that Nephi called to Zoram "in the voice of Laban" (1 Nephi 4:20), which could be called a stratagem. Remember back in Alma 43 when Captain Moroni was trying to outwit Zerahemnah? Captain Moroni "thought it no sin that he should defend [the Nephites] by stratagem" (Alma 43:30). In other words, it's not a sin to trick an enemy when you're trying to stop him from killing your family and putting you in bondage.

Stratagems, decoys, and distractions are tools of war. Satan especially likes to use them in his war against those who are trying to follow God.

In fact, everything I've read convinces me that Satan works more by distraction than confrontation.

➡ **Observation:** When it comes to spiritual things, God doesn't work by stratagems. He doesn't trick us into being spiritual. He doesn't use deception to get us to say our prayers or to do our home teaching. He invites, persuades, and promises, but he doesn't deceive. Satan, on the other hand, uses all kinds of tricks to entice us to leave our spirituality behind and follow him into a trap.

Satan is often called the master deceiver. He knows the tricks of his trade. The scriptures describe

Satan's tactics as traps, snares, lies, and stratagems. Sometimes he flatters us into thinking we can handle anything, and we get caught in our own snare. ◄■

Don't Do What David Did

The more I ponder Alma 52, the more I am reminded of the tragic Old Testament story of King David. One evening when David was walking around on his rooftop patio he saw Bathsheba bathing. He may have thought, "This isn't really a temptation. I just want to know who she is. Then I'll go back inside." He should have stayed in his stronghold, far away from the temptation, but he didn't. Elder Neal A. Maxwell has taught, "Where the impulse to do wrong appears, act against that impulse while the impulse is still weak and while the will is still strong" ("The Stern but Sweet Seventh Commandment," *New Era,* June 1979, 42).

David allowed himself to replay and reconsider the temptation until the temptation became stronger than his will to resist. Eventually he sent for Bathsheba. After he met her he should have sent her home and gone back to his stronghold. But he allowed himself to be lured further and further away until he broke the law of chastity. Later Bathsheba told David that she was pregnant. David, attempting to cover his sin, sent for Bathsheba's husband, Uriah, who was out fighting for his country. David was hoping that Uriah would spend the night with his wife, but Uriah refused, sleeping instead on King David's porch. So David sent Uriah to the worst part of the war, where he was killed (2 Samuel 11).

Eventually the Lord sent the prophet Nathan to confront David and make him acknowledge what he had done. What a sad story! David thought he wanted something, but he got nothing and lost everything. Goliath was no problem for David, but David's own curiosity and lust proved to be a more powerful enemy, and David left his stronghold. The following quote fits perfectly the message of Alma 52. President James E. Faust warned:

> Over my lifetime, I have seen some of the most choice, capable, and righteous of men stumble and fall. They have been true and faithful for many years and then get caught in a web of stupidity and foolishness which has brought great shame to themselves and betrayed the trust of their innocent families, leaving their loved ones a legacy of sorrow and hurt. My dear brethren, all of us, young and old, must constantly guard against the enticements of Satan. . . . We must choose wisely the books and magazines we read, the movies we see, and how we use modern technology, such as the Internet ("Be Not Afraid, Only Believe," *Ensign,* November 1997, 45).

Perhaps the message of Alma 52 is, "When the children of Lehi are successful, do what they did! When they're not successful, don't do what they did!" Maybe the battle for Mulek is intended to help us learn from the mistakes of others. In this case we learn from the mistakes of the ancient Lamanites, fellow members of the house of Israel.

Famous Last Words: "I'll Be Right Back"

Satan will try to flatter us out of our strongholds. He'll tempt us to think, "I'm going to leave activity in the Church just for a while, but I'll be back." While working on this book, I had the opportunity to speak to some young single adults at Utah Valley State College. I told them how the story in Alma 52 taught me the importance of not leaving my stronghold. I was delighted to receive the following e-mail from a single adult sister a few days later:

> I loved hearing about not leaving your stronghold! I am at a point right now in my life where I am trying to figure what all this staying righteous stuff is doing for my life. I know that it is the only way to be, but sometimes I wonder what all the times at the temple, time in my scriptures, time praying, time serving, and time trying to be so faithful is getting me! This last week I have been joking with some friends that I was going to take a break from the Church for a little while. It was great to hear you talk about not leaving your stronghold, not even for just a minute, and then come back. I know that I am what I am because of the gospel, and I know that I do all the "right" things because I love the Lord. I also know that His timetable is so different from mine! I am plugging along, knowing that my time will come and knowing that I am NOT going to leave my stronghold! I will hold on tight! That will be my STRATEGY!

Satan tries his deadly enticements on many LDS young people. Some young men have thought, "I can flirt with a little temptation now, but I'll be back. I'll repent later and go on a mission." Some young women have thought, "I can do what I want now, repent later, and still get married in the temple." Some have been flattered out of their strongholds by thinking that a "swimsuit edition" or a lingerie catalog is a small temptation—only to be lured later to pornography or worse. Others have thought that trying a little beer at a party is no big deal—only to end up experimenting with other types of alcohol and eventually drugs. The terrible reality is that what seems like a small temptation may be a deadly decoy that will lure us much further away than we initially intended to go. As a result, we may never get back to our place of safety.

I love Alma 52. It has taught me to look at every "small" temptation as a decoy. It has helped me to realize that when I'm tempted to compromise just a little, I should be shaking down to my bones! When I see something alluring, it should give me the creeps! When I'm flattered into thinking I can handle small temptations, I should keep up my guard! This chapter shows that there's an enemy out there who may be trying to "stratagem" me. Is this the message that Mormon intended us to get from Alma 52? I don't know. Perhaps. In any case, it's a good message and a valid warning of how Satan will use stratagems against us.

Let's move on to Alma 53. The city of Mulek was back in Nephite hands, and the Nephites had taken many Lamanite prisoners. But the armies of the Nephites were spread a little too thin. Where could they look for help? Who would step up? Answer: the youth. Many people say that the young people of today don't have any heroes. Not so for Latter-day Saints. In the next chapter, we get about two thousand of them.

Lessons from Alma 52

1. Don't leave your stronghold.
2. Small temptations may lure you into bigger temptations.
3. God doesn't trick us into being righteous.
4. When you're tempted, realize that someone may be trying to *stratagem* you!

CHAPTER 10

ALMA 53

Knowing What Is True, Being True to What You Know

The Lamanite prisoners are used to fortify the city Bountiful—
Dissensions among the Nephites give rise to Lamanite victo-
ries—Helaman takes command of the two thousand stripling
sons of the people of Ammon (ALMA 53 HEADNOTE).

With the city of Mulek back in Nephite hands and the
number of Lamanite prisoners of war increasing, Moroni
used the prisoners to build fortifications around the city of
Bountiful. However, all was not well. The Nephites had lost
many other cities. Mormon reported, "Because of iniquity
amongst themselves, yea, because of dissensions and
intrigue amongst themselves they were placed in the most
dangerous circumstances" (Alma 53:9).

Here They Come to Save the Day

From these "dangerous circumstances," we are introduced to the stripling warriors. The stripling warriors were

Lamanites by birth—the children of those converted by the missionary Ammon who had buried their weapons of war and taken an oath not to fight. For their protection, these Lamanite converts were invited to live with the Nephites. These converts had many sons who had not taken the oath, and they were willing to help the Nephites.

These two thousand young men took a different oath, an oath that sounded much like the oath the Nephites took under the title of liberty: "to fight for the liberty of the Nephites, yea, to protect the land unto the laying down of their lives; yea, even they covenanted that they never would give up their liberty, but they would fight in all cases to protect the Nephites and themselves from bondage" (Alma 53:17).

Because these two thousand wanted Helaman to be their leader, they are often referred to as the "sons of Helaman." The verses that describe these young men are marked with red pencil in millions of copies of the Book of Mormon:

> And they were all young men, and they were exceedingly valiant for courage, and also for strength and activity; but behold, this was not all—they were men who were true at all times in whatsoever thing they were entrusted. Yea, they were men of truth and soberness, for they had been taught to keep the commandments of God and to walk uprightly before him (Alma 53:20–21).

Knowing, Doing, Becoming

These two thousand young men knew the gospel was true, and they were true to the gospel! The lesson for us is obvious: If you know the Church is true, be true to the Church!

One day when she was in junior high school, my future wife, Kim, was walking around with a friend. The two of them were approached by a young man who asked, "Are you guys Mormon?" Kim's friend, who apparently was afraid of looking uncool, said, "No." Kim looked at her in surprise and then told the young man, "Well, I am." Her friend suddenly changed her story and said, "Just kidding. I am too."

"Just kidding Mormons" and "Marginal Mormons" might know the Church is true, but they might not be true to the Church. They might go to Church, but they might not be "into" the Church.

≋ **Mini Lesson:** Being spiritual doesn't mean just knowing things. It means knowing and doing. The wonderful thing about knowing and doing is that it starts another process. When you *know* what is right and you *do* what you *know*, you begin to *become* something different than you were. You become converted. Elder Dallin H. Oaks observed, "The gospel challenges us to be 'converted,' which requires us to *do* and to *become. . . .* We all know someone who has a strong testimony but does not act upon it so as to be converted. For example, returned missionaries, are you still seeking to be converted, or are you caught up in the ways of the world?" ("The Challenge to Become," *Ensign,* November 2000, 33).

You've probably heard the story about the song "I Am a Child of God." The original lyrics were, "Teach me all that I must *know.*" Elder Spencer W.

Kimball gently suggested that the word *know* be changed to *do*. He understood that knowing *and* doing result in becoming and that putting our gospel knowledge into action helps us become not just convinced but also converted ("New Verse Is Written for Popular Song," *Church News*, April 1, 1978, 16). ≋

The bottom line? The miraculous survival of the stripling warriors did not come from their experience in battle—they had none. It came because they knew what was true, and they were true to what they knew.

Counsel for Today's Stripling Warriors

In the early years of World War II, President J. Reuben Clark Jr. gave powerful counsel to the youth of the Church who would soon serve in the defense of freedom. Notice his emphasis on being true to what they knew.

> To our young men who go into service, no matter whom they serve or where, we say live clean, keep the commandments of the Lord, pray to Him constantly to preserve you in truth and righteousness, live as you pray, and then whatever betides you the Lord will be with you and nothing will happen to you that will not be to the honor and glory of God and to your salvation and exaltation. There will come into your hearts from the living of the pure life you pray for, a joy that will pass your powers of expression or understanding. The Lord will be always near you; He will comfort you; you will feel His presence in the hour of your greatest tribulation; He will guard and

protect you to the full extent that accords with His all-wise purpose. Then, when the conflict is over and you return to your homes, having lived the righteous life, how great will be your happiness—whether you be of the victors or of the vanquished—that you have lived as the Lord commanded. You will return so disciplined in righteousness that hereafter all Satan's wiles and stratagems will leave you untouched. Your faith and testimony will be strong beyond breaking. You will be looked up to and revered as having passed through the fiery furnace of trial and temptation and come forth unharmed. Your brethren will look to you for counsel, support, and guidance. You will be the anchors to which thereafter the youth of Zion will moor their faith in man (Conference Report, April 1942, 96).

Wow, what a promise! My favorite part is, "You will return so disciplined in righteousness that hereafter all Satan's wiles and stratagems will leave you untouched." If you ask me, I believe that's at least a part of why we have the Book of Mormon war chapters—to help us recognize and defeat the stratagems of Satan.

Well, back to the story. The addition of two thousand righteous warriors was a big help. But the Lamanite prisoners, all of whom had to be fed, watched, guarded, and controlled, were a huge concern to Captain Moroni and a substantial drain on the Nephites' resources. Something big had to happen! Something big *did* happen. Stay tuned. It happened in Alma 54.

Lessons from Alma 53

1. When you know the Church is true, be true to the Church.
2. Being spiritual means knowing *and* doing.

CHAPTER 11

ALMA 54

Fear God More Than Armies

Ammoron and Moroni negotiate for the exchange of prisoners—Moroni demands that the Lamanites withdraw and cease their murderous attacks—Ammoron demands that the Nephites lay down their arms and become subject to the Lamanites (ALMA 54 HEADNOTE).

Warning: It is a federal offense to read other people's mail. Nevertheless, we get to read a couple of other people's letters in Alma 54. Ammoron, the new king of the Lamanites who succeeded his brother, Amalickiah, sent a message to Moroni indicating that he wanted to exchange prisoners. Moroni rejoiced at the suggestion since food was scarce. He wanted to feed his own armies rather than divide food between his people and the Lamanite prisoners.

The Nephites held only Lamanite men as prisoners, while the Lamanites held entire families. Moroni wanted all of these Nephite families back, and in his response to

Ammoron, Moroni told him that he had more to fear than just the Nephite armies.

This exchange of letters is so packed with passion and emotion that you'll really miss out unless you read every word in Alma 54. I'll just give you a few of my favorite verses and make a few comments.

Moroni doesn't pull any punches as he responds to Ammoron's initial request:

> Behold, we are prepared to receive you; yea, and except you withdraw your purposes, behold, ye will pull down the wrath of that God whom you have rejected upon you, even to your utter destruction. But, as the Lord liveth, our armies shall come upon you except ye withdraw, and ye shall soon be visited with death, for we will retain our cities and our lands; yea, and we will maintain our religion and the cause of our God (Alma 54:9–10).

> ≈ **Mini Lesson:** Moroni lets Ammoron know that he ought to fear God more than anything else. Moroni seems to be saying, "It's not my wrath you ought to fear but the wrath of God, which we will be happy to deliver unless you withdraw." Similarly we are told in modern scripture, "Fear not what man can do," and "You should not have feared man more than God" (D&C 122:9; 3:7). ≈

When Moroni wrote his letter to Ammoron, was he measuring his words? Was he beating around the bush? Was he trying to "win friends and influence people?" Read on: "But behold, it supposeth me that I talk to you concerning these things in vain; or it supposeth me that thou art a child of hell" (Alma 54:11).

Some may read those words and think, "Gee, Moroni, don't sugarcoat it. How do you really feel about this guy?" Others may think Moroni's words were a little too harsh. Some may even ask, "Would Jesus talk that way?"

Is Being Meek the Same As Being Weak?

Fortunately we are supplied with the answer, right in our scriptures. Open your Book of Mormon to Alma 54 and look at footnote "a" in verse 11. What do you see? It points you to John 8:44. What does that verse say? Well, in John 8:44, Jesus was talking to certain Jews who were plotting against him, and Jesus said (brace yourselves): "Ye are of your father the devil, and the lusts of your father ye will do." So there you go. Moroni said, "Thou art a child of hell." Jesus said, "Ye are of your father the devil." Pretty much the same thing, wouldn't you say?

> ➤ **Observation:** Being meek doesn't necessarily mean being a doormat. One definition of meekness is "great power under control." Moroni was direct and clear, and so was the Savior. They spoke the truth. The truth justifies the righteous, but "the guilty taketh the truth to be hard" (1 Nephi 16:2). Meekness isn't weakness. Or, as someone once said, "If you think being meek is weak, try being meek for a week." ◄

Moroni's last paragraph to Ammoron is a righteous warrior's final warning: "Behold, I am in my anger, and also my people; ye have sought to murder us, and we have only sought to defend ourselves. But behold, if ye seek to destroy us more we will seek to destroy you; yea, and we will seek our land, the land of our first inheritance" (Alma 54:13).

Wow! If you were writing a letter like that, how would you close? "Sincerely"? "Warm regards"? "Love, Moroni"? No. See Alma 54:14 for the answer (a little incentive to open your scriptures today).

You've Got Mail!

Ammoron received Moroni's letter and wrote back. Ammoron's response was about what you'd expect. He agreed to the prisoner exchange but attempted to justify the Lamanite aggression by saying that the Nephites had robbed the Lamanites of their right to the government. This excuse is used more than once in the Book of Mormon. To Ammoron, it's a birth-order thing going all the way back to the family of Lehi and Sariah. Since Laman was older than Nephi, Ammoron suggested that Laman's descendants should rule over Nephi's descendants, which is an odd thing to say since Ammoron and Amalickiah were both Nephites.

To me the most interesting part of Ammoron's letter is this: "And as concerning that God whom ye say we have rejected, behold, we know not such a being; neither do ye" (Alma 54:21). Next to this verse I wrote in my margin, "Oh my Korihor!" Remember him? Korihor seemed to say, "Hey, if I don't know there's a God, you can't possibly know it either" (Alma 30:48). Often in the Book of Mormon, non-believers counter the testimony of believers with a statement such as, "You can't *know* that; nobody *knows* that." Apparently, Ammoron thought just like Korihor.

How did Ammoron close *his* letter? With this interesting declaration: "And behold now, I am a bold Lamanite." Whoa, Ammoron, are you really a Lamanite? Hmmm. Just like we talked about in Alma 43, being a Nephite or a Lamanite became more a matter of affiliation and belief and less a matter of lineage and birth. Ammoron was the brother of Amalickiah, a Nephite who conspired to be king. Yet here he says, "I am a bold Lamanite." What does he mean? He means a Lamanite by belief, not by birth.

After the letters had been exchanged, Captain Moroni had some decisions to make. Would he go through with it? Would he allow the prisoner exchange? Or did he have something better in mind? Something that would allow him to get all the Nephite prisoners back without releasing the Lamanite prisoners to Ammoron, which would have strengthened Ammoron's army? The answer to these questions and more await us in Alma 55.

Lessons from Alma 54

1. Fear God more than man.
2. Meekness is not weakness.

CHAPTER 12

ALMA 55

Be Cautious That No Poison Is Administered among You

Moroni refuses to exchange prisoners—The Lamanite guards are enticed to become drunk, and the Nephite prisoners are freed— The city of Gid is taken without bloodshed (ALMA 55 HEADNOTE).

After Moroni received Ammoron's reply and read his justification for attacking the Nephites, he was even angrier. He then decided to get the Nephite prisoners back in his own way. Moroni searched among his men for a descendant of Laman—a Lamanite by *birth* this time. He finally found one, and his name was Laman (which fit rather nicely). He was a former servant of the king of the Lamanites who was murdered by Amalickiah and his men. Apparently, he escaped and came to live with the Nephites.

Whining for Wine

When it was evening, Laman and a small number of men approached the Lamanite guards outside the city of Gid, where the Nephite prisoners were being guarded. "Fear not," Laman said, "behold, I am a Lamanite. Behold, we have escaped from the Nephites, and they sleep; and behold we have taken of their wine and brought with us" (Alma 55:8).

Suddenly everyone wanted to be Laman's friend: "Give us of your wine, that we may drink; we are glad that ye have thus taken wine with you for we are weary." But Laman was smart. Rather than giving them the wine immediately, he furthered the deception by saying, "Let us keep of our wine till we go against the Nephites to battle." This made the guards want the wine even more, until finally they began to *whine* about the *wine*. "We are weary, therefore let us take of the wine" (Alma 55:9, 10, 11).

Now I guess there's something I don't know about wine. They were saying, "Give us the wine, for we are weary." We are *weary?* I don't get that. It was *wine,* not *Gatorade*—there were no electrolytes in there. But I've never touched the stuff, so I don't know. Anyway, Laman, resisting just enough to be convincing, finally said, "You may do according to your desires" and gave them the wine (Alma 55:12).

The weary guards drank the wine until they were merry, then drunk, then asleep. The stratagem worked! They got their alcohol, but they traded their agency and their ability to guard the Nephite prisoners.

≋ **Mini Lesson:** I think the Word of Wisdom is as much about agency as it is about health. Brother Joseph Fielding McConkie has written, "To be high on drugs is to be low on agency. It is to have surrendered the right to control and govern one's own actions" (*Understanding the Power God Gives Us: What Agency Really Means* [Salt Lake City: Deseret Book, 2004], 82). We did not surrender our agency in the war in heaven; in fact, we fought to keep it. Why should we give it away now? The lesson is clear: Beware of temptations that persuade you to surrender your agency—even when (and especially when) you're weary. ≈

Now Captain Moroni had a choice. The Lamanites were asleep, the Nephite prisoners were unguarded, and the city of Gid was his for the taking. (As you can imagine, retaking Gid would make the Nephites downright Giddy.)

How hard is it to kill sleeping drunks? Not hard at all. Moroni could have wiped them out, but he would not kill helpless men. It's just not sportsmanlike. More important, however, it went against the character of Captain Moroni to kill when killing wasn't necessary.

"The Nephites could have slain them. But behold, this was not the desire of Moroni; he did not delight in murder or bloodshed, but he delighted in the saving of his people from destruction" (Alma 55:18–19).

While You Were Sleeping It Off

Rather than killing those who were supposed to guard the Nephite prisoners, Moroni's men "cast in weapons of war unto the prisoners, insomuch that they were all armed" (Alma 55:16). (I'm not exactly sure how they did that. How do you "cast" a weapon of war to someone you're trying to help? "Okay, I'm going to throw you a javelin—here, catch!")

When the Lamanites woke up, "they beheld that they were surrounded by the Nephites without, and that their prisoners were armed within." That's probably when the Lamanites put their hands up in the air and pleaded for mercy, but Mormon used a wonderful understatement to describe the situation: "They found that it was not expedient that they should fight with the Nephites" (Alma 55:22, 23).

Moroni had done it. He had retaken Gid and liberated the Nephite prisoners while keeping all of his Lamanite prisoners. And he had done it all without shedding blood.

Stratagem Others As They Have Stratagemed You

I guess the Lamanites weren't very original when it came to stratagems. They later tried the same "Here, have some wine" trick on the Nephites many times, but it didn't work. Can't you just see that?

"Hey, Nephites, would you like some wine?"

"Uh, no thanks, guys, but that was a good try."

You can just see the Lamanites arguing among themselves as they walked away. "I told you that wouldn't work, you knucklehead!"

The Lamanites didn't just try to give the Nephites wine to get them drunk, they also tried to give them wine laced with poison to get them killed. But the Nephites wisely tested the wine on the Lamanite prisoners to see if it was poisoned. "And they were thus cautious that no poison should be administered among them; for if their wine would poison a Lamanite it would also poison a Nephite" (Alma 55:32). I used to go right past that verse, thinking, "Hmmm, that's good logic." But now I've discovered two important lessons in there. First, "Be cautious that no poison is administered among you."

> ➡ **Observation:** There are physical poisons, and there are spiritual poisons. Some poison the body; others poison the spirit. Television, movies, and videos are often laced with poison. The adversary is secretly trying to poison us, so we should be cautious that no poison is administered among us. ◄

Everyone knows that there's a lot of mindless junk on television. I've been clipping news articles about it for years: "Psychologists Recommend Less Television for Children" and "Doctors Suggest More Exercise Today, Less 'Entertainment Tonight.'" By contrast, you've never seen an article that says, "Most Americans Not Receiving the Daily Minimum Requirement of Game Shows" or "Television Talk Shows Essential to Mental Health." The problem is that some television is more than just empty and hollow; it's downright poisonous. One day I heard a quote on the radio that really surprised me. Not because of what it said but because of who said it:

> TV's poison. To grow up and not to have a sense of responsibility, to have everything taken care of, to be plopped in front of a television instead of being read to or talked to or encouraged to interact with other human beings is a huge mistake, and that's what happens to a lot of children.

Guess who said that? A Church leader? A psychologist? A TV evangelist? No, it was Madonna ("Madonna on Life Before and After Motherhood," *Redbook,* January 1997, 102). Friends, when Madonna becomes the voice of reason, it's time to take a hard look at ourselves. If a pop star thinks television is poison, what should we think?

Elder Joseph B. Wirthlin also used the word "poison" to describe modern media: "Some programs are filthy and evil and are poisoning the minds of God's children today" ("The Priesthood of God," *Ensign,* November 1988, 36). The scary thing about poison is that sometimes you can be poisoned without knowing it or poisoned "by degrees," as was Lehonti back in Alma 47.

This Poison Thing Could Mushroom Out of Control!

Elder Spencer J. Condie wrote about the dangers of "secret poison" in an article not about wine but about mushrooms. The observations he made are both fascinating and frightening:

> Among the poisonous mushrooms is . . . [one called the] "jack-o'-lantern" mushroom. The body reacts to its poison very quickly with violent nausea and vomiting. Because of this immediate reaction, the "jack-o'-lantern" is not fatal.
>
> A much more dangerous mushroom is . . . [called the] "destroying angel." Just one or two in a batch of two dozen can poison an entire family. Because it tastes like an edible mushroom and has no *immediate* effect, the victim keeps on eating. Then, six to

101

fifteen hours later, when it is digested and its poisons have entered the bloodstream, the victim experiences severe nausea and cramps and unquenchable thirst. Eventually it destroys the liver. There is no known antidote, and the fatality rate is about 90 percent.

. . . Just as there are different kinds of poisonous mushrooms, so are there different kinds of music, movies, and magazines that poison the spirits of men and women. Some of these poisons are very much like "jack-o'-lantern" mushrooms because their impact is so repulsive and objectionable that we immediately reject them.

But there are other kinds of music, movies, and magazines that work very much like the "destroying angel"; that is, at first we have no idea that what we are listening to or watching or reading is slowly and surely poisoning our very souls ("The Message: Mushrooms, Music, Movies, and Magazines," *New Era*, February 1990, 4).

What's the message here? I think it's this: Do what the Nephites did. *Be cautious that no poison is administered among you!* Some of our modern media are like "destroying angels" that seep into our system "by degrees" until we end up watching shows and buying CDs that our gift of the Holy Ghost would have evicted immediately.

Poison: An Equal-Opportunity Destroyer

Being cautious about poison is a powerful message, but there's another one in that verse: "If it would poison a

102

Lamanite, it would also poison a Nephite." That seems rather obvious, doesn't it? But what about spiritual poison? Can spiritual poison be bad for one person but okay for another? Can we say, "It's okay for me to see but not for you?" Can anyone believe that they're immune to movies that are "vulgar, immoral, violent, or pornographic"? (*For the Strength of Youth* [Salt Lake City: Intellectual Reserve, 2001], 17). Elder J. Richard Clarke taught:

> There is only one standard of moral decency. Any film, television show, music, or printed material unfit for youth is also unfit for parents. Those who rationalize acceptance of immoral material on grounds of maturity or sophistication are deceived ("To Honor the Priesthood," *Ensign*, May 1991, 42).

This is a sobering quote when you remember that Matthew 24:24 indicates that some of the "very elect" could be deceived in the last days. In a nutshell, if it will poison you it will poison me. If it will poison a child, it will poison an adult. If it will poison a Latter-day Saint from this country, it will poison a Latter-day Saint from another country.

On to Victory

Well, we're done looking at Alma 55. This all started when Ammoron sent Moroni a letter about wanting to exchange prisoners. When it was all over, Ammoron didn't get the prisoner exchange he wanted, he lost the city of Gid, he lost the hungover Lamanites guarding the city of Gid, he lost the Nephite prisoners, and he got nothing in return.

Needless to say, Ammoron didn't send Moroni any more letters.

Moroni did, however, get a letter from his friend Helaman that contained some pretty miraculous stories about two thousand young men and their mothers. We get to read this letter in Alma 56–58.

Lessons from Alma 55

1. "If you're high on drugs (or wine), you're low on agency."
2. Be cautious that no poison is administered among you.
3. If it will poison one person, it will poison another.

CHAPTER 13

ALMA 56

The Righteous Need
Not Fear Death

*Helaman sends an epistle to Moroni recounting the state of the
war with the Lamanites—Antipus and Helaman gain a great
victory over the Lamanites—Helaman's two thousand stripling
sons fight with miraculous power and none of them are slain*
(ALMA 56 HEADNOTE).

After receiving threatening letters from Ammoron in
Alma 54, Captain Moroni must have been happy to get a letter from Helaman and even happier with Helaman's reports
of how the war was going in his part of the land. We were
briefly introduced to the stripling warriors in Alma 53, but
now that we're in Alma 56 we get to see them in action.

Will They Fall for Another Decoy?

Helaman's two thousand joined forces with a Nephite
general named Antipus. (That name may sound familiar.
Back in Alma 46–47, Lehonti and his men took refuge on

mount *Antipas*—a little different spelling.) Antipus and Helaman wanted to entice the strongest and most numerous Lamanite army out of the city of Antiparah. How do you get an army to leave its stronghold? As we learned earlier, you lure it out with a stratagem. It worked in retaking Mulek in Alma 52, and perhaps Antipus and Helaman thought it might work for them too.

Helaman marched with his two thousand "little sons" (Alma 56:30) as if they were carrying provisions to a neighboring city, with Antipus and his army following not far behind. Helaman made sure to march near the city of Antiparah, within sight of its Lamanite spies. It worked! The Lamanite army left its stronghold and pursued Helaman's two thousand sons. Maybe the Lamanites thought, "Hey, they're just a bunch of teenagers. We can take them!"

The word "stripling," according to Webster's 1828 American Dictionary of the English Language (which appeared just two years before the Book of Mormon was published), means "a youth in the state of adolescence, or just passing from boyhood to manhood; a lad." So Helaman's "lads" fled northward to lure the Lamanites even farther away. The Lamanites didn't notice the army of Antipus behind them until a while later. In Helaman's words,

> And thus we did lead away the most powerful army of the Lamanites; yea, even to a considerable distance, insomuch that when they saw the army of Antipus pursuing them, with their might, they did not turn to the right nor to the left, but pursued their march in a straight course after us; and, as we suppose, it was their intent to slay us before Antipus

should overtake them, and this that they might not be surrounded by our people (Alma 56:36–37).

Do you have the picture in your mind? The two thousand stripling warriors are being chased by the Lamanites, who are being chased by the army of Antipus. The chase lasted all day long, until all three armies broke it off and camped for the night. In the morning, however, the chase resumed once again. But this time it was Helaman and his sons who dared not "turn to the right nor to the left lest they should" be overtaken (Alma 56:40).

≈ **Mini Lesson:** Temptation will follow you all of your life, whether you want it to or not. If you turn to the right or left, it could overtake you, so stay on the "strait and narrow path" and don't get lost in "broad" or "strange" roads (1 Nephi 8:20, 32; 12:17). The Lord explained to Joseph Smith, "For God doth not walk in crooked paths, neither doth he vary from that which he hath said, therefore his paths are straight, and his course is one eternal round" (D&C 3:2). ≈

The chase continued all day and into the evening. Again the armies camped for the night. (I guess no one wanted to fight in the dark.) When Helaman and his two thousand warriors arose the next morning, they saw the Lamanites coming after them again. Suddenly, however, the Lamanites halted their pursuit and disappeared. Helaman didn't know what had happened. Were they overtaken by Antipus? Were they setting a trap for the stripling warriors?

Fear? Not!

How I wish my Book of Mormon came with video clips! I wish I could see Helaman address the two thousand warriors when suddenly their assignment changed! Rather than serve any longer as a decoy, Helaman's sons were about to do something they'd never done before. They were preparing to attack:

> Behold, we know not but they [the Lamanites] have halted for the purpose that we should come against them, that they might catch us in their snare; therefore what say ye, my sons, will ye go against them to battle? (Alma 56:43–44).

Helaman described the stripling warriors' response to his question: "And now I say unto you, my beloved brother Moroni, that never had I seen so great courage, nay, not amongst all the Nephites" (Alma 56:45). Let's think about that! "All" the Nephites? Is "all" a fairly high percentage? These young Lamanite converts were unmatched in their faith and bravery, even when compared to the Nephites. Listen to what else they said: "Behold our God is with us, and he will not suffer that we should fall; then let us go forth" (Alma 56:46).

Helaman observed, "Now they never had fought, yet they did not fear death" (Alma 56:47). How is that possible? These two thousand warriors had never fought before and were about to go up against the strongest, most numerous army of the Lamanites, yet they had no fear, even of death. What had they done to become so fearless?

≈ **Mini Lesson:** The antidote for fear (even fear of death) is all the things we've been taught: faith, repentance, and obedience. This should come as no surprise to us. Repenting and keeping covenants give us peace in this life and even peace in death. As we've been taught, "If ye are prepared ye shall not fear" (D&C 38:30). ≈

Alma the Younger, who spent three days in an unconscious state contemplating what it would be like to stand before God, often confronted his listeners with questions related to the fear of death. For example: "Could ye say, if ye were called to die at this time, within yourselves, that ye have been sufficiently humble? That your garments have been cleansed and made white through the blood of Christ, who will come to redeem his people from their sins?" (Alma 5:27). Here's another example: "Can ye look up to God at that day with a pure heart and clean hands?" (Alma 5:19).

Alma also spoke in sobering, frightening words about those who do not repent and are therefore not prepared to face God:

> For our words will condemn us, yea, all our works will condemn us; we shall not be found spotless; and our thoughts will also condemn us; and in this awful state we shall not dare to look up to our God; and we would fain be glad if we could command the rocks and the mountains to fall upon us to hide us from his presence (Alma 12:14).

The stripling warriors were faithful, obedient, and

prepared. If they died in battle, they could be as confident as the prophet Enos, who spoke about dying and meeting God without fear: "Then shall I see his face with pleasure," which sounds a lot nicer than hoping you'd be covered by rocks and mountains (Enos 1:27). Yes, the stripling warriors were prepared for battle and for death, but they didn't become prepared by themselves. They had been taught.

The Mother of All Victories Started with Mothers

Some of these verses in Alma 56 are well known, and you've heard them before. Chances are you hear these scriptures just about every Mother's Day. I want you to hear them again, but this time I want you to notice not only what the verses say but also what they don't say: "Yea, they had been taught by their mothers, that if they did not doubt, God would deliver them. And they rehearsed unto me the words of their mothers, saying: We do not doubt our mothers knew it" (Alma 56:47–48).

You can almost imagine the prophet Mormon abridging these records and thinking, "Families and motherhood will be under attack in the last days. I think I'll tell them about the power of mothers." You'll notice that the stripling warriors didn't say they'd been taught by their schoolteachers or seminary teachers or Sunday School teachers. We sustain those teachers and we're grateful for them, but the Book of Mormon teaches us that the best teaching happens at home. Elder Neal A. Maxwell taught this truth beautifully:

> When the real history of mankind is fully disclosed, will it feature the echoes of gunfire or the

shaping sound of lullabies? The great armistices made by military men or the peacemaking of women in homes and in neighborhoods? Will what happened in cradles and kitchens prove to be more controlling than what happened in congresses? When the surf of the centuries has made the great pyramids so much sand, the everlasting family will still be standing, because it is a celestial institution, formed outside telestial time ("The Women of God," *Ensign*, May 1978, 10–11).

Someone might ask, "Hey, where were their fathers all this time?" Good question. Alma 56:27 gives us the answer. Helaman reports, "There was brought unto us many provisions from the fathers of those my two thousand sons." Fathers bringing *provisions* reminds us of the father's primary role as a *provider*. Next to Alma 56:27, I made my own footnote to the Proclamation on the Family:

> By divine design, fathers are to preside over their families in love and righteousness and are responsible to provide the necessities of life and protection for their families. Mothers are primarily responsible for the nurture of their children. In these sacred responsibilities, fathers and mothers are obligated to help one another as equal partners ("The Family: A Proclamation to the World," *Ensign*, November 1995, 102).

Interesting, isn't it? Alma 56 shows us something similar to the divine roles outlined in the Proclamation on the

Family—mothers who teach and nurture and fathers who provide (see also D&C 83:2–4).

Here They Come to Save the Day!

Okay, we've got to finish the story. The Lamanites were no longer chasing the stripling warriors. Helaman didn't know where the Lamanites were, but he thought they might have been forced to turn around and fight with Antipus and his forces.

Helaman asked his troops if they were ready to face the Lamanites, and the two thousand warriors courageously responded, "Let's go get 'em" (or more accurately, "Let us go forth"). The battle was about to begin.

When the two thousand warriors came around the bend, they saw what Helaman had suspected. "The armies of Antipus had overtaken [the Lamanites], and a terrible battle had commenced" (Alma 56:49). Antipus and his army were in deep trouble. They were weary because of their long march, and Antipus and many of the Nephite leaders had fallen. This gave the Lamanites courage, and they were pursuing the army of Antipus with great vigor when suddenly (you can almost hear the bugle sound "charge!") "Helaman came upon their rear with his two thousand, and began to slay them exceedingly, insomuch that the whole army of the Lamanites halted and turned upon Helaman" (Alma 56:52).

Aha! Now that the Lamanites were facing the stripling warriors, the army of Antipus had time to regroup. Once they did, they attacked the Lamanites from the rear. The Lamanites were surrounded, fighting the stripling warriors on one side and the remainder of the army of Antipus on the other side. The battle raged until the Lamanites were compelled to surrender and deliver themselves up as prisoners. After the surrender, Helaman began a head count of his warriors, fearing that many of them had been killed.

> But behold, to my great joy, there had not one soul of them fallen to the earth; yea, and they had fought as if with the strength of God; yea, never were men known to have fought with such miraculous strength; and with such mighty power did they fall upon the Lamanites, that they did frighten them; and for this cause did the Lamanites deliver themselves up as prisoners of war" (Alma 56:56).

Things were going well in the war effort, but the Nephites' growing success also brought growing numbers of Lamanite prisoners, and guarding them all was a growing problem. Then things got even more interesting. Helaman received a letter—a letter from Ammoron, the king of the Lamanites.

Lessons from Alma 56

1. The righteous need not fear death.
2. The best teaching happens at home.

CHAPTER 14

ALMA 57

Some Were About to Give Way, Some Were Firm and Steadfast

Helaman recounts the taking of Antiparah and the surrender and later the defense of Cumeni—His Ammonite striplings fight valiantly and all are wounded, but none are slain—Gid reports the slaying and the escape of the Lamanite prisoners (ALMA 57 HEADNOTE).

Helaman and Antipus had succeeded in luring the most numerous army of the Lamanites out of the city of Antiparah and then beating it in battle. Afterward the Nephites were once again hip deep in Lamanite prisoners. When the dust had settled, Helaman read the epistle he had received from Ammoron. Ammoron was looking for a deal. A large number of Lamanites had become prisoners of war, and Ammoron's armies were shrinking. Ammoron offered to give the city of Antiparah back to the Nephites if the Nephites would release their Lamanite prisoners. (The

Nephites had lured the Lamanite army out of Antiparah, but a few Lamanites remained inside the city).

Helaman wrote back, telling Ammoron that he was sure his forces were strong enough to take Antiparah by force and that he would only release the Lamanite prisoners if Ammoron would release the Nephite prisoners. Ammoron refused, so Helaman made preparations to attack Antiparah. Evidently those occupying the city of Antiparah knew the Nephites were about to attack, and they fled. Continuing his report to Moroni, which began in Alma 56, Helaman said, "And thus the city of Antiparah fell into our hands" (Alma 57:4). Needless to say, Ammoron didn't send Helaman any more letters.

In the meantime, Helaman received six thousand more men, as well as sixty more sons of the people of Ammon.

Delivery for the Lamanites—Please Sign Here

The next city Helaman wanted to recapture was called Cumeni. This time, rather than luring the Lamanites out of the city, they starved them out. Here's what happened: Helaman and his forces surrounded Cumeni by night. Inside the city, meanwhile, the Lamanites were expecting supplies from Lamanite headquarters. "At length their provisions did arrive, and they were about to enter the city by night," Helaman reported. "And we, instead of being Lamanites, were Nephites; therefore, we did take them and their provisions." Without their provisions, the Lamanites in Cumeni couldn't last long. Not many days later, they "yielded up the city unto our hands" (Alma 57:10, 12).

A Nice Problem But a Problem Nevertheless

The Nephites had taken too many Lamanite prisoners during the past few battles. Helaman had to use nearly all of his force to guard them. They had to be fed, and every once in a while they revolted. So Helaman assigned a Nephite commander named Gid to take a small army and march the Lamanite prisoners down to Zarahemla. Gid and his army were gone only a day, however, when suddenly they were back—without the prisoners they were supposed to take to Zarahemla! Helaman had no time to ask what had happened because a Lamanite army was also back, attacking with a vengeance.

The Empire Strikes Back

Ammoron had sent a numerous army of Lamanites back into battle, and the Nephites were once again fighting for their lives. Helaman told Moroni:

> But behold, my little band of two thousand and sixty fought most desperately; yea, they were firm before the Lamanites, and did administer death unto all those who opposed them. And as the remainder of our army were about to give way before the Lamanites, behold, those two thousand and sixty were firm and undaunted. Yea, and they did obey and observe to perform every word of command with exactness; yea, and even according to their faith it was done unto them; and I did remember the words which they said unto me that their mothers had taught them (Alma 57:19–21).

When the battle was over, Helaman once again ordered a head count to determine Nephite losses. He reported the

116

results of the head count to Moroni in these words, "To our great astonishment, and also the joy of our whole army, there was not one soul of them who did perish; yea, and neither was there one soul among them who had not received many wounds" (Alma 57:25).

The front cover of this book features a painting by Clark Kelley Price titled *It's True Sir—All Present and Accounted For*. It illustrates this story from Alma 57.

> ❦ **Major Lesson:** Some were "about to give way"; some were "firm and undaunted." These words describe the Nephite armies, but they also describe members of the Church today. While some are "firm and undaunted," others are "about to give way" to the world. Some Latter-day Saints refuse to go to worldly movies; some "give way" and see them. Some refuse worldly fashions; some "give way" and wear them. Here's the scary part—in the war chapters, what happened to those who gave way? The firm and undaunted were only wounded, but those who gave way were often killed. ❦

So why were the 2,060 successful? "They did observe to perform every word of command with exactness." Today's "word of command" could be our *For the Strength of Youth* pamphlet. President Ezra Taft Benson taught, "You are to be the royal army of the Lord in the last days. You are 'youth of the noble birthright.' (*Hymns,* 1985, no. 255.) In the spiritual battles you are waging, I see you as today's sons of Helaman" ("To the 'Youth of the Noble Birthright,'" *Ensign,* May 1986, 43).

Unfortunately some are not firm and undaunted. They may say, "I don't see what's wrong with this music, I don't see what's wrong with *Austin Powers,* I don't see what's wrong with wearing tight or revealing clothes." Is that following the Lord's command with exactness? Is that being firm in the faith? About as firm as a noodle in a rainstorm. Latter-day Saints have been sent to change the world, but too many are letting the world change them. To this group, the war chapters ask this pointed question: Are you a warrior or a sheep? A soldier in the battle against evil or just another of the thoughtless creatures who follow the false shepherds of the world? (see S. Michael Wilcox, *Don't Leap with the Sheep* [Salt Lake City: Deseret Book, 2001], 74).

Okay, there's something in here we need to be careful about. Commenting on the fact that none of the 2,060 stripling warriors was killed, Helaman said, "And we do justly ascribe it to the miraculous power of God, because of their exceeding faith in that which they had been taught to believe—that there was a just God, and whosoever did not doubt, that they should be preserved by his marvelous power" (Alma 57:26).

Faith in Whom?

The faith of the stripling warriors kept them from dying. Sometimes, however, people of great faith die. Sometimes people are given priesthood blessings and they still die. And often, we think to ourselves, "Oh, if only I had more faith, they would have lived." That is not necessarily true. Abinadi had great faith, but he died. Joseph Smith had great faith, but he died. Hundreds of other examples could be cited, perhaps even involving people you know.

➤ **Observation:** Faith is not willing your own desires into existence. It's not concentrating on some result or believing in something you want with all your might, trying to make it come true. The first principle of the gospel is not faith in ourselves and in what we desire but faith in the Lord Jesus Christ and in *his* will. When we exercise faith in *him,* and in *his* timing, we can be assured that all things will work together for our good, however painful they may be for us at the moment. If someone you love dies, it does not necessarily mean that your faith was lacking. It may just mean that for reasons we may not know in this life, it was the Lord's will that the person pass on. One day we will understand why! (D&C 101:32–36). Real faith is knowing that the Lord loves us with all of his heart so we can trust in him with all of our hearts. One day he will explain all things and wipe away all of our tears. ◀

The stripling warriors survived the battle for Cumeni because of their faith in God and because, in this case, it was God's will that they survive.

We Won, But We Wound up Wounded
(say that fast ten times)

Another interesting thing we can learn from this story is this: Notwithstanding their great faith, all of the stripling warriors were wounded—*all* of them.

119

≋ **Mini Lesson:** Having a testimony and having great faith in Christ does not guarantee that we won't suffer. Abraham, Job, Abinadi, Nephi, Joseph Smith, and countless other righteous people we could mention all suffered. Jesus Christ suffered beyond them all, and he never did anything wrong. As someone once said, "In this life, suffering is mandatory, but misery is optional." We're all going to go through some tough times; that's just the nature of life on earth. But our tough times cannot destroy our hope unless we let them. That is our option. We're all going to suffer, but we don't have to be miserable. Since all of the stripling warriors were wounded, we might expect that we'll also get some bumps and bruises as we go through life's battles. ≋

A Not-So-Funny Thing Happened on the Way to Zarahemla

Okay, back to the story. When the battle for Cumeni was over and the dead of the Nephites and Lamanites were buried, Helaman asked Gid what happened to the Lamanite prisoners he was taking to Zarahemla. Gid explained that on the way to Zarahemla, a Nephite spy approached them and excitedly reported a pending Lamanite invasion of Cumeni. The Lamanite prisoners overheard and revolted, running upon the swords of the Nephites. Most of them were slain, but the rest escaped. Fortunately, however, Gid returned with his men just in time to help repel the Lamanite attack.

Had the Lamanite prisoners not escaped, Gid and his men would not have been there to help Helaman.

Gid concluded his report to Helaman with gratitude and humility: "And behold, we are again delivered out of the hands of our enemies. And blessed is the name of our God; for behold, it is he that has delivered us; yea, that has done this great thing for us" (Alma 57:35). Here's another reason to admire Moroni, Helaman, Gid, and the other chief captains. They always gave the credit for their success to God!

President Abraham Lincoln warned Americans that they should also remember God and not believe that their prosperity was their own doing:

> We have been the recipients of the choicest bounties of Heaven. We have been preserved these many years in peace and prosperity. We have grown in numbers, wealth and power. . . . But we have forgotten God. We have forgotten the gracious Hand which preserved us in peace, and multiplied and enriched and strengthened us; and we have vainly imagined, in the deceitfulness of our hearts, that all these blessings were produced by some superior wisdom and virtue of our own. Intoxicated with unbroken success, we have become too self-sufficient to feel the necessity of redeeming and preserving grace, too proud to pray to the God that made us (in *America's God and Country,* comp. William J. Federer [Coppell, Texas: FAME Publishing, 1994], 383–84).

Captain Moroni, Helaman, Gid, and even Abraham

Lincoln were humble enough to know that they should acknowledge God's hands in all things (D&C 59:21).

An Earlier Manti Pageant

The Nephites had retaken Antiparah and Cumeni. But they soon learned, as we all do, that whatever we obtain, we have to maintain, and the Nephite forces were spread rather thin in keeping those cities. However, Helaman had another city in his sights named Manti. He wanted it back. How should he take it? Would another decoy work? Decoys had worked before, but had the Lamanites learned to recognize decoys? Had the Lamanite commanders issued an order to their forces saying, "Hey, you boneheads, the next time a small Nephite army takes off running, *don't chase 'em!*"? The answer to this question and more awaits us in Alma 58.

Lessons from Alma 57

1. Some were firm and undaunted; others were about to give way.
2. Real faith is faith in Christ and in his will.
3. Having faith in Christ doesn't mean we won't ever suffer.
4. Acknowledge the hand of God in all things.

CHAPTER 15

ALMA 58

God Will Visit the
Faithful with Assurances

*Helaman, Gid, and Teomner take the city of Manti by a strat-
agem—The Lamanites withdraw—The sons of the people of
Ammon are preserved as they stand fast in defense of their liberty and faith* (ALMA 58 HEADNOTE).

Alma 58 is the last part of Helaman's letter to Moroni
(the letter began in Alma 56).

Man, Oh Manti

Helaman wanted to retake the city of Manti, but he
and the other chief captains were convinced that the
Lamanites would not fall for another decoy. They also
knew that it would be a mistake to attack them while they
were in their strongholds. In addition, the Nephites were
spread so thin in maintaining the cities they'd already
retaken that those who were available to fight would be
greatly outnumbered. So the best strategy, they decided,

was to wait. Waiting was difficult, however. In the last part of his letter to Moroni, Helaman said, "We did wait in these difficult circumstances for the space of many months, even until we were about to perish for the want of food" (Alma 58:7).

Too Little Too Late

Finally two thousand more men and provisions arrived, but Helaman knew it was not enough to go up against an innumerable army of Lamanites. He had already sent word to the governor of the land that the Nephites needed more assistance, and yet they received little help.

They were low on men but high on fear. So where did they turn for peace? They turned to God. They did the only thing they could do. They prayed: "Therefore we did pour out our souls in prayer to God, that he would strengthen us and deliver us out of the hands of our enemies, yea, and also give us strength that we might retain our cities, and our lands, and our possessions, for the support of our people" (Alma 58:10).

> ≈ **Mini Lesson:** Have you ever felt like Helaman? Have you ever felt like saying, "I can't do this by myself; I need help"? Have you ever prayed and worried and stressed over a personal problem for *many months* before you finally got an answer? Me too. I've met teenagers who are deeply concerned about a friend or a family member who is falling away. They want help immediately. They want a solution "right now." They want to know what words to say

that will "fix" things on the spot. I've even had teenagers give me a tape recorder or a mailing address, requesting me to say just the right thing or write the perfect words to someone and solve their problem in an instant. I've always felt pretty helpless and inadequate in those situations. Sometimes answers to problems are slow in coming. One of the hardest things for all of us to learn, young or old, is patience. We don't want to be patient. We want what we want when we want it. But sometimes the Lord makes us wait.

I guess that's why I love these verses. Where should we turn when we feel helpless, worn out, used up, or undersupplied? Read these words from the hymn "How Firm a Foundation" for an answer:

> When through fiery trials thy pathway shall lie,
> My grace, all sufficient, shall be thy supply.
> I'll strengthen thee, help thee, and cause thee to stand—
> Upheld by my righteous, omnipotent hand.
> (*Hymns of The Church of Jesus Christ of Latter-day Saints* [Salt Lake City: The Church of Jesus Christ of Latter-day Saints, 1985], no. 85) ≈

Helaman reminds us that we should keep believing, keep praying, and keep trusting, even after waiting for help for "many months." We'll do what we can do, and then God's grace, all sufficient, will be our supply (Moroni 10:32).

God Answers Prayers

What was the result of Helaman's prayer?

> Yea, and it came to pass that the Lord our God did visit us with assurances that he would deliver us; yea, insomuch that he did speak peace to our souls, and did grant unto us great faith, and did cause us that we should hope for our deliverance in him (Alma 58:11).

Isn't that a nice verse? Look at the key words: assurance, peace, faith, hope, and deliverance. Renewed in hope and in spirit, Helaman once again focused on the city of Manti.

One More Time!

Helaman had a plan. First he took his forces and camped near the city walls. The Lamanites sent their spies out of Manti to "discover the number and the strength of [their] army" (Alma 58:14). After discovering that the Nephite force was small, the Lamanites began to prepare an attack.

Seeing the Lamanite preparations, Helaman put another stratagem into motion. Perhaps Helaman hoped the Lamanites would fall for a decoy one more time. He ordered Gid and Teomner to take a small number of men and hide on both sides of Helaman's camp. Eventually "the Lamanites [came] out with their numerous army" against Helaman (Alma 58:18). And what did Helaman's army do? Take a wild guess—they took off running into the wilderness, and the Lamanites pursued them with "great speed." In fact, they went so fast after Helaman that they didn't even notice Gid and Teomner hiding in the bushes (Alma 58:19).

After the Lamanite army passed by, Gid and Teomner "did rise up from their secret places, and did cut off the spies of the Lamanites that they should not return to the city." Then they ran to the city and "fell upon the guards who were left to guard the city, insomuch that they did destroy them and did take possession of the city" (Alma 58:20–21). Whoa, that was too easy! Helaman explained that the Lamanites "did suffer their whole army, save a few guards only, to be led away into the wilderness" (Alma 58:22).

Another problem remained, however. Manti was theirs, but a huge army was pursuing Helaman and his 2,060 warriors. Helaman, however, knew what he was doing. Rather than just run somewhere into the wilderness, he retreated toward Zarahemla, which caused the Lamanite commanders to suspect that they were being led into a trap. So the Lamanites gave up the chase, turned around, and started back toward Manti. But first they stopped to camp for the night. Oops.

Helaman's men could have set up camp also, but they didn't. They stayed awake. And while the Lamanites slept, the stripling warriors marched by another route back to the city of Manti.

≋ **Mini Lesson:** One of my favorite quotes comes from Henry Wadsworth Longfellow: "The heights by great men reached and kept were not attained by sudden flight, but they, while their companions slept, were toiling upward in the night." The stripling warriors' night march also reminds me of this profound observation from an anonymous source: "Jesus chose his disciples when they were working; Satan chooses his when they're idle." ≈

I love Helaman and the stripling warriors not only because they were faithful but also because they *worked*. Faith and works make a powerful combination. They wanted Manti more than they wanted rest. It was mind over mattress.

Hi, Honey, We're Home

A day or two later the Lamanites returned to the city of Manti (looking well rested, we suspect). To their great surprise, they saw the Nephites *inside* the city. I wonder if the Nephites called to the Lamanites and said, "Hey guys, what took you so long?" The Lamanites were "astonished exceedingly and struck with great fear, insomuch that they did flee into the wilderness" (Alma 58:29).

How do you conquer a force that's much bigger than you? You lure them out of their stronghold into the wilderness, and then you capture their stronghold while they sleep. Helaman did it! He was outnumbered and undersupplied, but he took the city of Manti without the shedding of blood.

Mission Accomplished

Can you imagine how happy it must have made Captain Moroni to receive this report from Helaman? "And those cities which had been taken by the Lamanites, *all of them* are at this period of time in our possession; and our fathers and our women and our children are returning to their homes" (Alma 58:31, emphasis added).

Helaman was brilliant, but he never took credit for his accomplishments on the battlefield. He told Moroni, "We trust in our God who has given us victory over those lands" (Alma 58:33).

The Nephites still had plenty of things to be concerned about, however. Their armies were small, too small to maintain their cities, and Helaman knew it. And he continued to wonder why they hadn't received more reinforcements from the government. In the final part of his letter to Moroni he nailed it on the head: "We fear that there is some faction in the government, that they do not send more men to our assistance" (Alma 58:36).

If Moroni enjoyed Helaman's letter, he didn't enjoy it for long. Huge problems had arisen at home, and many Nephites were falling by the sword. We read what Captain Moroni was dealing with on the home front in Alma 59.

Lessons from Alma 58

1. God will visit us with assurances when we're under-supplied.
2. There is no substitute for faith combined with work.

CHAPTER 16

ALMA 59

Better to Prepare and Prevent
than Repair and Repent

Moroni asks Pahoran to strengthen the forces of Helaman—The Lamanites take the city of Nephihah—Moroni is angry with the government (ALMA 59 HEADNOTE).

After Captain Moroni received Helaman's epistle, he immediately wrote to the governor of the land, Pahoran, requesting that Helaman be sent additional men. While Helaman was successful in regaining control of the cities in his quarter of the land, Captain Moroni was having a more difficult time.

Of particular concern was the city of Nephihah. Captain Moroni sent additional manpower to Nephihah, "knowing that it was easier to keep the city from falling into the hands of the Lamanites than to retake it from them" (Alma 59:9). Okay, hold everything. Did you catch that? Let's read it again: *"knowing that it was easier to keep the city from falling into the hands of the Lamanites than to retake it from them."*

Do you see the lesson in there? It's a good one, so let's stop and spend some time on it.

⊗ **Major Lesson:** Let's apply Captain Moroni's principle to our personal battles with sin. We might say it this way: "It is easier to keep yourself from falling into sin than to repent and regain your worthiness." President Ezra Taft Benson taught the same principle: "When it comes to the law of chastity, it is better to prepare and prevent than it is to repair and repent" (*The Teachings of Ezra Taft Benson* [Salt Lake City: Bookcraft, 1988], 285). Satan tries to make sin look enticing, fun, or adventurous. But he doesn't tell you about the hellish consequences of sin. President Harold B. Lee said, "The more I see of life, the more I am convinced that we must impress you young people with the awfulness of sin rather than to content ourselves with merely teaching the way of repentance. I wish that someone could warn you of the night of hell that follows the committing of a moral sin or of a beastly act (*The Teachings of Harold B. Lee,* ed. Clyde J. Williams [Salt Lake City: Bookcraft, 1996], 225).

We all know that repenting of serious sin is possible, but it can be very difficult and painful. Satan doesn't mention that part either. President Spencer W. Kimball taught, "We must remember that repentance is more than just saying, 'I am sorry.' It is more than tears in one's eyes. It is more than a half a dozen prayers. Repentance means suffering. If a person hasn't suffered, he hasn't repented. I don't care how many times he says he has. If he hasn't suffered, he hasn't repented. He has got to go through a change in his system whereby he suffers and then forgiveness is a possibility. Nobody can be forgiven unless there is adequate repentance. You bishops remember that, will you! The Savior can do almost anything in the world, but he can't forgive somebody who hasn't repented (*The Teachings of Spencer W. Kimball,* ed. Edward L. Kimball [Salt Lake City: Bookcraft, 1982], 99).

Echoing President Kimball, Elder Henry B. Eyring has counseled, "Teach the people that repentance hurts" (*To Draw Closer to God* [Salt Lake City: Deseret Book, 1997], 52). These statements should motivate us to stay as far away from sin as possible. I hope we'll come away from Alma 59 "fortified," knowing that it is better to keep ourselves from falling into sin than it is to go through a painful repentance process to regain our worthiness. ◈

Back to the story. Despite Moroni's preparations, the city of Nephihah was lost. The Lamanite army was so numerous that the fortified city was overcome. This was a cause of great sorrow to Moroni and his chief captains. But Nephihah was not lost because of inadequate fortifications, poor planning, or flawed military strategy.

What Is Their Problem?

The Nephites had been told time and time again that if they kept the commandments they would prosper in the land. Once again we learn that their problem was not superior Lamanite military aggression; rather, it was inferior Nephite spiritual preparation. Hugh Nibley put it this way:

> No matter how wicked and ferocious and depraved the Lamanites might be (and they were that!), no matter by how much they outnumbered the Nephites, darkly closing in on all sides, no matter how insidiously they spied and intrigued and infiltrated and hatched their diabolical plots and breathed their bloody threats and pushed their formidable preparations for all-out war, *they were not the Nephite problem.* They were merely kept there to remind the Nephites of their real problem, which was to walk uprightly before the Lord (*Since Cumorah,* in *The Collected Works of Hugh Nibley,* 2d ed., 14 vols. [Salt Lake City and Provo, Utah: Deseret Book and the Foundation for Ancient Research and Mormon Studies, 1988], 7:339–40).

Brother Nibley, of course, made his comments hundreds of years after the Nephite wars had ended. But Moroni and his chief captains also knew exactly what the real problem was at the time.

> And now, when Moroni saw that the city of Nephihah was lost he was exceedingly sorrowful, and began to doubt, because of *the wickedness of the people,* whether they should not fall into the hands of their brethren. Now this was the case with all his chief captains. They doubted and marveled also because of *the wickedness of the people,* and this because of the

success of the Lamanites over them (Alma 59:11–12; emphasis added).

We've seen a lot of letters exchanged during the past few chapters: Moroni to Ammoron (Alma 54), Ammoron to Moroni (Alma 54), Helaman to Moroni (Alma 56–58), Ammoron to Helaman (Alma 57), and, at the beginning of this chapter, Moroni to chief judge or governor Pahoran (Alma 59). Moroni was about to send a second letter to Pahoran, and if you think the tone of some of his previous letters was a little, well, *intense,* you ain't seen nothin' yet. As you know, Moroni and Pahoran were both Nephites. They weren't enemies; they were on the same side! Yet Moroni's letter to Pahoran after the fall of the city of Nephihah is perhaps the most scathing letter of them all. We get to read it in Alma 60.

Lessons from Alma 59

1. It's better to prepare and prevent than to repair and repent.
2. Nephite wickedness caused the Nephites more problems than Lamanite aggression.

CHAPTER 17

ALMA 60

Cleanse the Inner Vessel

Moroni complains to Pahoran of the government's neglect of the armies—The Lord suffers the righteous to be slain—The Nephites must use all of their power and means to deliver themselves from their enemies—Moroni threatens to fight against the government unless help is supplied to his armies (ALMA 60 HEADNOTE).

Helaman had retaken many cities from the Lamanites, but his forces were spread too thin. Moroni had recently lost the city of Nephihah and had seen many Nephites slain. With these things weighing heavily on him, Moroni wrote a letter to Pahoran.

Moroni's description of the situation is pretty bleak:

> And now behold, I say unto you that myself, and also my men, and also Helaman and his men, have suffered exceedingly great sufferings; yea, even

hunger, thirst, and fatigue, and all manner of afflictions of every kind. But behold, were this all we had
suffered we would not murmur nor complain (Alma
60:3–4).

Moroni could handle the hunger, thirst, fatigue, and
afflictions. His complaint was about the government's
neglect.

I Can't Stand All This Sitting

Apparently, Moroni pictured Pahoran and the others at
the head of the government sitting around in ignorance of
all the fighting and dying going on in other parts of the land.
Moroni makes it clear in his letter that he didn't like sitting
around, and he didn't like thrones.

> Can you think to sit upon your thrones in a state
> of thoughtless stupor, while your enemies are spread-
> ing the work of death around you? . . . Behold could
> ye suppose that ye could sit upon your thrones, and
> because of the exceeding goodness of God ye could
> do nothing and he would deliver you? . . .
> Or do ye suppose that the Lord will still deliver
> us, while we sit upon our thrones and do not make
> use of the means which the Lord has provided for us?
> Yea, will ye sit in idleness while ye are surrounded
> with thousands of those, yea, tens of thousands, who
> do also sit in idleness, while there are thousands
> round about in the borders of the land who are
> falling by the sword, yea, wounded and bleeding?
> (Alma 60:7, 11, 21, 22).

In my scriptures, next to Alma 60:22, I have the words "Dad in the Pacific." Here's why: My father told me a story once that I will never forget. He served aboard the *USS Saratoga,* the largest aircraft carrier in America's fleet during World War II. He told me that one night someone on the ship picked up a California radio station.

Do They Know What We're Going Through Out Here?

What the men way out on the other side of the Pacific Ocean heard on the radio that night probably made them feel neglected, unappreciated, and perhaps a little angry. They heard Eddy Duchin and his orchestra broadcasting from the Sir Walter Raleigh Hotel in San Francisco. In the background, they heard dancing, laughter, and the tinkling of champagne glasses. My father and his buddies thought, "Do they know what we're going through out here while they're at home dancing and partying?"

My father and his buddiess were a little upset because of what had happened on their ship on a day earlier—February 21, 1945. The *USS Saratoga* was covering the U.S. invasionof Iwo Jima when it came under attack. My dad was nineteen at the time. In his words, here's what happened:

> I had taken my place on lookout watch at about 1600 hours (4 P.M.). The day was Wednesday, February 21, 1945.
>
> I had been on lookout watch for about an hour when our lookout leader advised me to proceed to my battle station, as bogeys [unidentified aircraft] had

shown up on our radar screen at 80 miles. I immediately left my lookout station, descended through the superstructure, and was crossing under the flight deck to the port side when I heard, "Boing, boing, boing." This was the general quarters alarm.

I sprang into a dead run, as did all the other sailors, and as I arrived at my battle station, our starboard guns began firing, while at the same time, the ship was jolted heavily as I heard loud explosions. I suddenly realized that this was the real thing—we were under attack. As I joined my gun crew, they were breaking out ammunition furiously. I took my place as second loader and began to pass clips of 40-millimeter ammo to the first loader. At this time, the gun captain yelled out, "You second loaders, if the first loader gets hit, drag him off and get up there and take his place."

Fright began to overtake me as I realized the possibility of death had become very real. I immediately thought of Mom and Pop. I could see them opening a telegram from the Navy Department informing them that their son had been killed in action. All this came to me in an instant. I could hear the whine of the electric motors on the gun as they started up. By now, many guns, both port and starboard, were firing, even the five-inches. (Our five-inch guns were for long range, our 40-mm guns were for intermediate range, and our 20-mm machine guns were for short range.)

At this moment, as I looked up and out across the water, I spotted a plane leveling off low on the water and coming directly at us. Thinking it was one of our F6F Hellcats, I started to say, as I pointed, "What's he doing?" All of a sudden our gun swung into position and began firing rapidly at it, as did all other guns on the port side. I then realized it was not one of ours—it was a Japanese Zeke! I pulled my helmet down tight on my head and began to pass ammunition as fast as I could.

At this time our 20-mm began firing, and then I knew that he was getting in close to us. I didn't have much time to be frightened—though I was. My main concentration was on passing those shells into the hands of the first loader in the right position so he could, without pausing, drop them into the breach of the gun. (The correct procedure here was critical.)

A few moments later the ship again was jolted heavily as a loud explosion followed. We were showered with pieces of teakwood and metal fragments. Heavy black smoke blew over us. By now every gun was firing rapidly. The noise was intense, and I had no cotton in my ears. I don't know if the plane I saw was the one that hit us or not.

At this time I again glanced out over the water, and I saw one of our destroyers coming across our bow at flank speed and firing every gun it had. Apparently the attacking aircraft were coming in from our starboard bow, and the destroyers were moving into position to protect our bow.

We had already taken several hits, and the entire

forward end of the flight deck was on fire. We continued firing, but at what, I don't know. The ship would quiver every few moments, and I realized we were really taking a beating. I could hear the water pumps start up as the firefighters began fighting the flames. Much water was being pumped aboard in an effort to douse the fires.

Again the ship was jolted, as though it had been blown entirely out of the water. Almost immediately, black smoke poured through the large ventilation fans from the hangar deck and onto our gun mount. We nearly choked. A suicide plane had crashed into the starboard side of the ship and had gone through to the hangar deck. A fire followed as some of our planes began to explode and burn.

Above and behind me, on the passageway, I could hear rapid footsteps and voices shouting, "Get out of the way!" I looked up momentarily and saw some men running toward the forward bow. They had left their guns in a state of sheer panic as a large twin-engine Japanese bomber was bearing down on us at the stern. Some men, however, remained on their guns and shot it down just before it got to us. If that bomber had made it through, he could have put our steering gear out of commission, and we would have been sitting ducks.

We were taking on water more rapidly now, and we began to list [tip] to starboard as the ship began losing speed. A lull in the firing ensued, and we were instructed to smear flash burn cream on our faces, necks, and the backs of our hands to protect us from any flashes from bombs or other explosions. . . .

By now we were dead in the water (stopped), and we all began to put on life preservers as some began to cut life rafts loose. I began to prepare for the worst. A terrible fright came over me as I thought of abandoning ship and having to jump into that cold, gray Pacific. I knew that at this time of year, a person would only last a few minutes there, even with a life preserver.

About this time, two jeep (small) carriers had come in our vicinity. Some Japanese suicide planes took after them and made direct hits on both of them. I saw them burning. Later, we got the news that they were both sunk. One of these was the *Bismarck Sea*. I can't recall the name of the other one.

Darkness began to overtake us now, and we again began to fire. I believe our guns were now being fired by radar.

The bilge pumps were finally started up, and now the water taken on to fight fires was being pumped overboard. A short time later, the ship began to slowly move forward. I began to feel somewhat relieved. At least we weren't sinking. We slowly picked up speed and, in a short time, were making at least seventeen knots.

[The next morning] I moved about on the ship assessing the damage. It was incredible. It was sickening. Some men had been blown to bits, and their flesh had to be hosed off the bulkhead and decks. The smell of burnt flesh turned my stomach, and I nearly vomited. As the dead were being counted, I wondered how some of my high school chums had fared. I knew a fire room on the starboard side had been hit, and I became concerned about Keith Crawford. I later learned that the fire room that was hit was the next one aft from his. Thank goodness. All the rest of my classmates were okay.

I learned that one tall, handsome, red-headed LDS boy from Provo died on a forward gun just below our lookout station. I learned that the Marine detachment we had had suffered extremely heavy losses. They manned 40-mm guns on the forward end of the flight deck, where most of the damage occurred. Some Marines had to go over the side or burn to death. Some were burned to death; many went over the side never to be found.

I was approached by someone to proceed to the bomb locker and help remove some badly burned bodies. I declined, as I'm sure the person who asked me could see my sickened condition and knew I would be of no use to him. I later learned that those bodies there were literally roasted, and if you tried to pick them up, they fell apart. They finally had to shovel them up ("Autobiography of Jack Lee Bytheway," unpublished manuscript).

That segment was a little long, but I wanted you to read it because my father's story has helped me understand why Captain Moroni was so angry. That kamikaze attack killed

CLEANSE THE INNER VESSEL

123 men and wounded 192. While the men on the *Saratoga* were fighting for their lives and for the freedom of their country, they may have remembered what they picked up on the radio—sounds of the people my dad and his buddies were fighting for dancing and laughing at a hotel ballroom. Some of my dad's friends died that day so that those at home could enjoy their freedom.

So I don't blame Moroni at all for the tone of his letter. He was fighting for the freedom of his country, he was surrounded by the death and destruction of his own people, and he thought the Nephite government back in Zarahemla was having a party.

I'm Going to Clean House

In his letter Moroni reminded Pahoran that "God has said that the inward vessel shall be cleansed first, and then shall the outer vessel be cleansed also" (Alma 60:23). This idea is repeated in the war chapters and in the Book of Mormon perhaps dozens of times. If the Nephites could fix their internal problems, the Lord would help them with their external problems (attacks from their enemies).

> ❀ **Major Lesson:** The war chapters teach us that we must individually "clean house"—get our spiritual lives in order. The outer vessel could be compared to our observable behavior—going to Church and seminary, saying our prayers, and so forth. But real power comes when our inner vessel is clean, when we're striving to repent and strip ourselves of pride, envy, jealousy, and unclean desires. Easier said than done?

Yup. But perhaps there's a reason this lesson is repeated so often in the Book of Mormon. We need it! 🕮

Moroni went so far as to say, "Send us relief, or we're coming after you!" (Alma 60:30). But Moroni wasn't after power. He didn't want to take over as governor. As we have seen, he wasn't interested in sitting on a governor's throne. Moroni's closing paragraph reminds us of his real motives:

> Behold, I am Moroni, your chief captain. I seek not for power, but to pull it down. I seek not for honor of the world, but for the glory of my God, and the freedom and welfare of my country. And thus I close mine epistle (Alma 60:36).

What do you think Pahoran thought when he read Moroni's 36-verse letter? How would he respond? Would he be offended? Would he tell Moroni he didn't know what he was talking about?

The problem is, there was something Moroni didn't know, something pretty unbelievable. Back in Zarahemla, the headquarters of the Nephite government, a new adversary was sitting on the throne, claiming to be king! And what's worse, he had just written a letter to Ammoron, the king of the Lamanites, hoping to form an alliance! "No way!" you say? Way. How in the world did that happen? The details are coming in Alma 61.

Lesson from Alma 60

1. Cleanse the inner vessel.

CHAPTER 18

ALMA 61
God Has Not Commanded Us to Be Subject to Our Enemies

Pahoran tells Moroni of the insurrection and rebellion against the government—The king-men take Zarahemla and are in league with the Lamanites—Pahoran asks for military aid against the rebels (ALMA 61 HEADNOTE).

Let's say you received a letter that basically said, "You're proud, you're lazy, you're neglecting your friends, you're a traitor, and I'm coming after you." How would you respond—especially if all the things you were accused of were untrue? You might be upset, resentful, and defensive. And you'd have a right to be. But just because you have the right to do something doesn't mean it's the right thing to do.

Thanks for Your Letter

You might not want to answer a letter like that, but Pahoran knew Moroni's heart, and he knew that Moroni didn't have all the facts. So Pahoran responded by immediately letting Moroni know where he stood: "Moroni, . . . I do not joy in your great afflictions, yea, it grieves my soul. But behold, there are those who do joy in your afflictions" (Alma 61:2–3).

Then he explained the incredible events in Zarahemla: "They have driven me out before them, and I have fled to the land of Gideon, with as many men as it were possible that I could get" (Alma 61:5). In other words, Pahoran had been kicked out of Zarahemla. (It's a good thing they forwarded his mail!) And guess who kicked him out? The kingmen! Yup, those guys were still around. It gets worse:

"They have got possession of the land, or the city of Zarahemla; they have appointed a king over them, and he hath written unto the king of the Lamanites, in the which he hath joined an alliance with him" (Alma 61:8).

The new king's name was "Pachus" (Alma 62:6). Pachus's plan was to hang on to Zarahemla until Ammoron and his Lamanite forces could come and conquer the remainder of the land. So, needless to say, Chief Governor Pahoran was dealing with all kinds of turmoil at home, and the last thing he needed was to be chewed out by his chief military man.

The Best Defense Is to Take No Offense

I believe that one of the best things about Alma 61 is Pahoran's answer to Moroni's blistering epistle, and I'm not alone. Elder Neal A. Maxwell called Pahoran's response "a classic in meekness and empathy!" (*A Wonderful Flood of*

Light [Salt Lake City: Bookcraft, 1990], 65). Here's my favorite part of Pahoran's reply:

> And now, in your epistle you have censured me, but it mattereth not; I am not angry, but do rejoice in the greatness of your heart. I, Pahoran, do not seek for power, save only to retain my judgment-seat that I may preserve the rights and the liberty of my people. My soul standeth fast in that liberty in the which God hath made us free (Alma 61:9).

What a great example. When something happens to us, we can either react or respond. Pahoran didn't react, he responded. If you look at the word *responsibility*, it's actually two words joined together—the ability to respond. Pahoran could have struck back with something like, "How dare you—you have no idea what we're going through up here." But instead, he said, "I rejoice in the greatness of your heart." Pahoran had the ability to respond.

Captain Moroni must have been relieved when he read these words. Although Moroni and his men were hungry and tired, at least they could rest assured that Pahoran was still with them. Not only that, but it was apparent that Pahoran still had some fight left in him as well. He continued:

> And now, behold, we will resist wickedness even unto bloodshed. We would not shed the blood of the Lamanites if they would stay in their own land. We would not shed the blood of our brethren if they would not rise up in rebellion and take the sword against us. We would subject ourselves to the yoke of bondage if it were requisite with the justice of God,

or if he should command us so to do. But behold he doth not command us that we shall subject ourselves to our enemies, but that we should put our trust in him, and he will deliver us (Alma 61:10–13).

Pahoran once again stated the Nephites' justification for taking up arms against the Lamanites, and he reaffirmed their trust in God.

We Know All about the Enemy of the Nephites—Who Is Our Enemy?

I love these words in Alma 61:13: "He doth not command us that we shall subject ourselves to our enemies, but that we should put our trust in him."

≈ **Mini Lesson:** The devil is "an enemy to all righteousness" (Alma 34:23), which means he's our enemy too. But if we trust God, he will help us conquer Satan. When someone does something wrong, he might jokingly say, "The devil made me do it." But the fact is, when we trust God, the devil can't *make* us do anything. Alma taught the people in Ammonihah that they would not be tempted beyond their ability to withstand, and he told them how that works: "Humble yourselves before the Lord, and call on his holy name, and watch and pray continually, that ye may not be tempted above that which ye can bear, and thus be led by the Holy Spirit, becoming humble, meek, submissive, patient, full of love and all long-suffering" (Alma 13:28).

"Humble yourselves" means we can't look at

temptations and say, "I can handle that." We've already seen the folly of that idea in previous chapters. Also, we're told to "call on his holy name," which obviously means to pray for strength. Next, we must "watch and pray," which means to watch—not just to look but to "watch" or guard like a night watchman. We must guard against temptation and watch so carefully that we recognize decoys and stratagems set to trap us. When we do these things, we are promised that we won't be tempted beyond what we can bear. ≈

The next time you feel tempted beyond your ability, remember the phrase, "God has not commanded us to be subject to our enemies, but to trust him!" We are not Satan's subjects. We are children of God.

Moroni, Here Are Your Orders

Pahoran gives Moroni new orders as part of his plan to retake Zarahemla and remove Pachus and the king-men.

> Therefore, come unto me speedily with a few of your men, and leave the remainder in the charge of Lehi and Teancum; give unto them power to conduct the war in that part of the land, according to the Spirit of God, which is also the spirit of freedom which is in them (Alma 61:15).

Wow, what a great statement! "The Spirit of God, which is also the spirit of freedom." God wants his people, all people, to be free. In one of my favorite movies, *The Ten Commandments*, Joshua says, "God made men. Men made slaves." It's true. God doesn't work by coercion, bondage, and slavery. He will force no one to heaven. He doesn't reign like a dictator. The Spirit of God is the spirit of freedom.

During his state of the union speech January 28, 2003, President George W. Bush said, "The liberty we prize is not America's gift to the world, it is God's gift to humanity." The Lord doesn't want his children to be slaves to other men. He also gives us commandments or standards for living, not to limit our freedom but to protect us from consequences. Following the standards of the Church will prevent us from losing our freedom and becoming slaves to worldly vices like alcohol, immorality, or pornography. The Lord knows that wickedness never was happiness, and he wants us to be happy.

> ➡ **Observation:** God gives us the freedom to choose, and with that freedom he wants us to choose the right. For example, some teenagers will say, "I can't see that movie," but the ones who are a little more spiritually mature say, "I don't want to see that movie," or "I choose not to see that movie." One day these teenagers will be old enough to buy alcohol or see any movie they want. Then they will have the opportunity to choose the right when choosing the wrong is also an option. That is when their spiritual maturity will really shine. ◀

Oh Yeah? Well Same to You, Buster

Now it's time for Pahoran to close his letter. He wanted freedom for the Nephites, as did Moroni, and Pahoran's

letter closes not with a "same to you" but with these sup-
portive, inspiring words:

> See that ye strengthen Lehi and Teancum in the
> Lord; tell them to fear not, for God will deliver them,
> yea, and also all those who stand fast in that liberty
> wherewith God hath made them free. And now I
> close mine epistle to my beloved brother, Moroni
> (Alma 61:21).

Isn't that great? Pahoran closes his letter by referring to
Moroni as "my beloved brother." Elder Maxwell was right;
this letter really is a "classic in meekness and empathy."
Moroni must have been thrilled that he had been wrong
about Pahoran.

> ≈ **Mini Lesson:** People we love and admire might
> be wrong from time to time. Even people at Church
> get things wrong. It may be that like Moroni, they
> simply don't have all the facts. That's okay. We've
> been wrong before too, and we hope people will for-
> give us when we say something before we have all the
> facts. Pahoran teaches us that we should still treat
> those who might misunderstand us as our beloved
> brothers and sisters. ≈

I've Got to Raise an Army, March to Gideon, Conquer the King-men—I'm Swamped!

Moroni had to leave Lehi and Teancum on their own.
But they were competent generals, and they would be fine.
But Moroni was going to need a large army. He was going

to need to do some recruiting on his way to meet Pahoran in Gideon. Moroni may have had some other things on his mind too. Not only did Moroni need to retake Zarahemla, but he also needed to retake Nephihah as well. In fact, Moroni had several major tasks on his to-do list:

- Raise an army
- March to Gideon
- Join Pahoran's army
- Conquer the king-men
- Retake Zarahemla
- Retake Nephihah
- Get much-needed supplies to Lehi and Teancum

And I thought I had a lot to do. Do you think Moroni will check all of these off? Well, has he ever let us down before? You won't want to miss what happens next. See you in Alma 62.

Lessons from Alma 61

1. God does not command us to be subject to our enemies.
2. The Spirit of God is the spirit of freedom.
3. People make mistakes, but they are still our brothers and sisters.

CHAPTER 19

ALMA 62
Respond to Afflictions with Faith

Moroni marches to the aid of Pahoran in the land of Gideon—
The king-men who refuse to defend their country are put to
death—Pahoran and Moroni retake Nephihah—Many
Lamanites join the people of Ammon—Teancum slays
Ammoron and is in turn slain—The Lamanites are driven
from the land, and peace is established—Helaman returns to
the ministry and builds up the Church (ALMA 62 HEADNOTE).

Moroni received Pahoran's letter and was simultaneously
filled with joy and sorrow—joy because Pahoran was not a
traitor but was faithful to God and the cause of freedom, and
sorrow because the king-men in Zarahemla had rebelled
against their country and their God. After giving Lehi and
Teancum command of the army, Moroni and a small number of men made their way toward Gideon, raising the standard of liberty and building an army to restore Pahoran to
the judgment seat.

And it came to pass that thousands did flock unto his standard, and did take up their swords in the defense of their freedom, that they might not come into bondage (Alma 62:5).

Moroni arrived in Gideon, joined with Pahoran and his army, and "went down with their armies into the land of Zarahemla, and went forth against the city, and did meet the men of Pachus" (Alma 62:7). Mormon doesn't tell us much about the battle, only the end result: "Pachus was slain and his men were taken prisoners, and Pahoran was restored to his judgment-seat" (Alma 62:8).

Treason Is a Capital Offense

It's impossible to overstate the trouble the king-men caused. Think of the number of Lamanite and Nephite lives lost because of the pride of those who wanted a king! All of the war chapters we've covered have one thing in common—the wars they discuss occurred because evil, prideful men wanted to abolish freedom and enthrone a king, and they persuaded others to follow them. Zerahemnah, Amalickiah, Ammoron, and the king-men caused all of the death and destruction outlined in Alma 43–62.

When you view the war chapters as a whole and think about the terrible things that happened, you understand why the Nephites had to do what they did next:

Those men of Pachus and those king-men, whosoever would not take up arms in the defence of their country, but would fight against it, were put to death. And thus it became expedient that this law should be strictly observed for the safety of their country; yea, and whosoever was found denying their freedom was speedily executed according to the law (Alma 62:9–10).

Moroni restored freedom and order in Zarahemla, but he had not forgotten his comrades in arms back at the front. He "immediately caused that provisions should be sent, and also an army of six thousand men should be sent unto Helaman," and he sent "six thousand men, with a sufficient quantity of food," to Lehi and Teancum (Alma 62:12–13).

Next on Moroni's list was to recapture the city of Nephihah. On the way there, however, Moroni encountered "a large body of men of the Lamanites" (Alma 62:15). Once again they engaged in battle. When the hostilities were over, four thousand Lamanite survivors entered a covenant of peace and were mercifully sent to dwell with the people of Ammon—the parents of the stripling warriors.

Hey, How Did You Guys Get in Here?

Moroni moved his armies near the city Nephihah and camped for the night. The armies of the Lamanites had no desire to come out and fight the large Nephite army, so they stayed within the city walls. When it was night, Moroni "came upon the top of the wall" and surveyed the situation below. He discovered that the Lamanites were all camped by the east wall at the entrance, and they were all asleep. So Moroni's army prepared ladders and strong cords and let themselves down into the city on the west side (Alma 62:20–23).

When the Lamanites awoke and discovered the Nephite army within the walls, they began to flee. Many were slain and taken prisoner, many others escaped, and ultimately the city of Nephihah was taken without the loss of one Nephite.

Something interesting happened when the battle was over. Many Lamanite prisoners didn't want to go home. Like the other Lamanites mentioned above, they wanted to join the people of Ammon and "become a free people" (Alma 62:27). Apparently, living under the apostate Nephite King Ammoron wasn't an appealing choice. The Lamanites wanted freedom.

◈ **Major Lesson:** The United States of America has a lot of problems, and we all know it. But if you ever want to know if a system of government is good or bad, there's a simple question you can ask: If there were no borders, no border guards, and no control on immigration in a particular country, would people run in or run out? When it comes to the United States, the answer is incredibly obvious: People would run in. In fact, even with border guards and all the rest, people *do* run in, often risking their lives in the process. So when Hollywood celebrities and countless others make negative statements about our system of government, ask yourself, "Are people drowning off the coast of Cuba trying to escape Florida?" No way. But many have drowned off the coast of Florida trying to escape Cuba. The value of freedom—freedom of religion, freedom of worship, and freedom from kings and tyrants—is one of the greatest lessons from the war chapters. Make sure you don't miss it. 🕸

Moroni was a freedom-loving, merciful man. So the Lamanites who wanted to live in freedom with the people of Ammon were allowed to do so.

Farewell to a Valiant Warrior

Next, Moroni moved his armies toward the land being defended by Lehi and Teancum. When the Lamanite armies saw Moroni coming, they fled until they met Lehi and Teancum and their armies. The entire Lamanite army was in one body, and their king, Ammoron, was with them. Because of their prolonged marches, the Lamanite and Nephite armies camped for the night. One of the Nephite commanders, however, couldn't sleep.

> [Teancum] was exceedingly angry with Ammoron, insomuch that he considered that Ammoron, and Amalickiah his brother, had been the cause of this great and lasting war between them and the Lamanites, which had been the cause of so much war and bloodshed, yea, and so much famine (Alma 62:35).

So Teancum, as he had done before in Alma 51, crept by night into the camp of the Lamanites in search of the king. Teancum eventually found Ammoron and "cast a javelin at him, which did pierce him near the heart" (Alma 62:36). Way back in Alma 51:34, when Teancum slew Amalickiah, he "*put* a javelin to his heart." In Ammoron's case, however,

Teancum "*cast* a javelin at him"—an important difference because Ammoron was not instantly killed but was able to awaken his servants before he died, "insomuch that they did pursue Teancum, and slew him" (Alma 62:36).

When Moroni and Lehi heard the news, they were devastated. Teancum was their friend and comrade, a righteous warrior with whom they had fought side by side. I wish we knew more about him. The few references we have to Teancum seem to indicate that he had endured many trials. Mormon summarized his life in these words: "He had been a man who had fought valiantly for his country, yea, a true friend to liberty; and he had suffered very many exceedingly sore afflictions. But behold, he was dead, and had gone the way of all the earth" (Alma 62:37).

The Final Battle of the War Chapters

The next morning Moroni and his huge armies came upon the Lamanites and drove them out of their lands. Mormon concludes the war chapters with these words: "And thus ended the thirty and first year of the reign of the judges over the people of Nephi; and thus they had had wars, and bloodsheds, and famine, and affliction, for the space of many years" (Alma 62:39). How many years? When we began the war chapters in Alma 43, it was the eighteenth year of the reign of the judges; this final battle concluded in the thirty-first year. That means the Nephites had been at war for thirteen years.

Counting the Cost

How would thirteen years of war affect the Nephites? Imagine the emotional turmoil associated with the loss of life. They say that in peacetime sons bury their fathers, but in wartime fathers bury their sons. We suspect that many families lost brothers, fathers, and husbands, leaving many widows and orphans behind.

Famine is another side effect of war, since those who are normally doing the planting, cultivating, irrigating, and harvesting of crops have left their farms to go off to battle. In addition, cities, roads, and other structures have to be rebuilt or repaired. These are a few of the physical effects of war.

What would the spiritual impact be? How would the people's attitudes and feelings about God be affected? The Book of Mormon tells us the spiritual impact of these thirteen years of war:

> Many had become hardened, because of the exceedingly great length of the war; and many were softened because of their afflictions, insomuch that they did humble themselves before God, even in the depth of humility (Alma 62:41).

❧ **Major Lesson:** Some were hardened, and some were softened. Why the difference? We each have a choice of how we will respond to trials. Some people move away from God when times are tough; others move closer to God. Laman and Lemuel lived in the same family, traversed the same desert, and suffered the same afflictions as Nephi and Sam, but their response to their trials was totally opposite—Laman and Lemuel became hardened, while Nephi and Sam became softened.

I have a dear friend named Kathy Schlendorf who

159

was involved in a terrible car accident. Among her other injuries, her pelvic bone was broken in six places. When she finally went home from the hospital, she had to use a walker to get around. Her nearly two-year-old son, not understanding his mother's medical condition, started whining one morning for his breakfast. She didn't want to wake her husband, so, with the aid of her walker, she moved across the kitchen toward the cupboards. When she was finally within reach, she realized that she would fall if she lifted either hand off the walker to open the cupboard. A feeling of helplessness and despair overcame her, and she lowered her head and burst into tears. Who could blame her?

Suddenly, Kathy felt the Spirit speak to her, and it said something like this: "Kathy, you are a physical wreck. You can be a physical wreck *and* an emotional wreck, or you can just be a physical wreck." In a moment of anguish, Kathy learned a powerful lesson that some people never learn, and the lesson is this— you have a choice. Yes, you may have every right to be irritated, uptight, and upset, but you still have a choice. In that wonderful yet painful moment, my friend Kathy chose to be happy. She was well aware that she was a physical wreck, but she chose to be happy, cheerful, and joyful in attitude and spirit.

To this day, Kathy is one of the most delightful, selfless, affirming people I've ever known. How did she get that way? Is it because she has no trials? No. She's endured plenty. It's because with the help of

God, Kathy learned that she had a choice. She could become hardened or softened. Kathy has been a great example to me, and when I find myself becoming grouchy or bitter about things, I remind myself that if Kathy could choose to be happy in her circumstances, perhaps I can choose to be happy in mine. ◈

All Right, Folks, Show's Over—Back to Your Homes and Places of Business

At the close of Alma 62, Moroni retired to his house and gave the command of his armies to his son Moronihah. Pahoran returned to the judgment seat in Zarahemla. Helaman, who had so successfully led the stripling warriors through many battles, returned to his duties as the Lord's prophet among the people by declaring the word of God and establishing the church throughout the land.

The Nephites prospered, multiplied, and grew strong. But they did not forget one all-important thing:

> But notwithstanding their riches, or their strength, or their prosperity, they were not lifted up in the pride of their eyes; neither were they slow to remember the Lord their God; but they did humble themselves exceedingly before him. Yea, they did remember how great things the Lord had done for them, that he had delivered them from death, and from bonds, and from prisons, and from all manner of afflictions, and he had delivered them out of the hands of their enemies. And they did pray unto the Lord their God continually, insomuch that the Lord did bless them, according to

his word, so that they did wax strong and prosper in the land (Alma 62:49–51).

They prospered and they grew, but this time they remembered God. Usually, when people in the Book of Mormon prosper, they begin to forget God, but this time, after a thirteen-year period of war and hardship, they remembered— at least for a while.

    ❇ **Major Lesson:** Don't ever forget to remember. Elder Spencer W. Kimball made an important comment about the word *remember.* He said, "When you look in the dictionary for the most important word, do you know what it is? It could be 'remember.' Because all of you have made covenants—you know what to do and you know how to do it—our greatest need is to remember" ("Circles of Exaltation," in *Charge to Religious Educators,* 2d ed. [Salt Lake City], 28 June 1968). That single quote has really had an impact on my Book of Mormon study. You'll find the word *remember* and its opposite, *forget,* throughout the Book of Mormon. When the people are righteous, a verse will read something like this: "And they remembered the Lord their God." When the people are wicked, a verse will say something like this: "And they did not remember." Every Sunday we go to Church, and what do we do? We make a solemn covenant to "always remember him." ❇

Sometimes the Lord allows people to suffer all sorts of problems just to get them to remember him. Today we're living in a time of terrorism. Notice the word *terror* in the following verse from Helaman:

> And thus we see that except the Lord doth chasten his people with many afflictions, yea, except he doth visit them with death and with terror, and with famine and with all manner of pestilence, they will not remember him (Helaman 12:3).

Every Sunday we make covenants to remember. We're told to read our scriptures daily. Why? To help us remember what great things the Lord has done for our fathers. We're told to have family prayer and personal prayer every day. Why? One reason is to help us remember God and our dependence on him. So much of what we do spiritually is to help us keep the Lord in our hearts and thoughts. I hope we can remember God without having to go through the things the Nephites did.

Now What?

Now that we've plowed through all of these chapters, what do we do with all of the things we've learned? Can we put these lessons into some bite-size pieces? We'll try to summarize some of the wonderful messages from the war chapters next.

Lessons from Alma 62

1. Freedom is worth fighting for.
2. We can be hardened or softened by trials; we choose our response.
3. Don't forget to remember God.

CHAPTER 20

Aftermath

The introduction to this book mentions some of the reasons the Book of Mormon might contain so many chapters about war. First, the war chapters help us spiritually by giving us insight into how we can successfully battle sin and temptation. Second, the war chapters help us live in the last days, a time of "wars and rumors of war." This chapter reviews these reasons and summarizes some of the lessons we can learn from them.

Satan is at war with all that is "virtuous, lovely, or of good report or praiseworthy" (Articles of Faith 1:13). He is ruthless, and he is relentless, but the Book of Mormon helps us prepare to battle him. Here are some of my favorite spiritual lessons from the war chapters.

Spiritual Lessons from the War Chapters

1. Repent first, prepare second. The major message of the war chapters can be summarized in one word—repent.

We must cleanse the inner vessel, get our spiritual lives in order, and then prepare for the spiritual or temporal battles that may come. Moroni consistently tried to prepare the people spiritually before they made swords and built fortifications. He knew that if they were spiritually prepared, God would help them fight their battles.

2. Prepare for attacks on your faith. After the Nephites repented, they prepared themselves, working feverishly for coming attacks. They did simple but important things, like preparing heaps, timbers, pickets, and towers. We can do the same thing by remembering prayer, scripture study, and service to others. We can attend our meetings to renew our covenants and strengthen each other. Most important, we can do what the Nephites did—listen to the watchmen on the tower, the living prophets who can see danger coming from far away.

As I studied the war chapters, I underlined, highlighted, and scribbled many words in the margins. Here are some words I came up with that describe the Nephites when they were successful:

- Prepared (spiritually and temporally)
- Mindful (they remembered their covenants)
- Busy (building fortifications and marching during the night)
- Responsible (for failures)
- Grateful (to God for successes)
- Discerning (of stratagems and poisons from the Lamanites)
- Respectful (for life on both sides)

Each of these words describes important things we can do to prepare for our personal battles against temptation.

3. Be wary of Satan's stratagems. The word *stratagem* has not been a part of my everyday vocabulary—until now. Since I began studying the war chapters, *stratagem* has become one of my favorite words to describe how Satan tries to destroy us. The similarity between the stratagems of war and the stratagems Satan uses against us is fascinating. I really believe that's at least partly why the war chapters have been preserved for us—to teach us about Satan's stratagems.

God doesn't deceive us into being righteous, but Satan uses all kinds of deceptions to try to destroy our spirituality. Here are some words I scribbled in my scriptural margins to describe why the Lamanite armies failed:

- Distracted (not doing nothing but doing something else)
- Decoyed (going after small numbers and being pulled into traps)
- Lured (out of a stronghold)
- Flattered (out of a stronghold)
- Enticed (out of a stronghold)
- Power hungry (apostate Nephites who wanted to be king)
- Bloodthirsty (apostate Nephite commanders who did not care for the blood of their own people)

Elder Richard G. Scott observed, "Satan has a powerful tool to use against good people. It is distraction" ("First Things First," *Ensign,* May 2001, 7).

We can learn from the war chapters that the adversary

will never stop his distractions, decoys, and snares. More specifically, we can remember that Satan will entice us to come down from higher ground, or to come down from our "mountain." We can recognize the clever lie that ultimately killed Lehonti: "You can come down just a little and still be in control." We can recall that Satan will attempt to poison us "by degrees" until we are spiritually dead. When we reflect on how the Nephites retook the cities of Mulek, Antiparah, and Manti, we can remember to constantly guard against the enticements of Satan and never allow ourselves to be flattered, lured, or distracted out of our stronghold.

Ephesians 6:11 tells us to "put on the whole armour of God, that ye may be able to stand against the wiles of the devil." I've always liked that scripture, but I didn't know what "wiles" meant, so I looked up the word in Webster's 1828 dictionary. I was excited when I saw its definition: "A trick or stratagem practiced for ensnaring or deception; a sly, insidious artifice." Wow! Doesn't that totally fit the war chapters? We could restate Ephesians 6:11 this way: "Put on the whole armour of God, that ye may be able to stand against the *stratagems* of the devil."

In the future, if we ever come across a "small" temptation, if we're ever enticed or distracted to leave our stronghold, or if we ever think, "I can handle this and I'll be right back," I hope we will shudder with the realization that someone may be trying to *stratagem* us. We need to look over our shoulder and watch our back because we'll be dealing with Satan's temptations and stratagems as long as we live.

4. Be faithful, not fearful. The war chapters teach us not to dwell on the harsh, difficult things in life. When we're living the gospel, we, like the stripling warriors, have little to fear, including death. I am so grateful for President Gordon B. Hinckley, our modern-day watchman on the tower. He is well aware of world events. He knows what's going on and how bad things are, yet he always sets an example of optimism:

> The war goes on. It is waged across the world over the issues of agency and compulsion. It is waged by an army of missionaries over the issues of truth and error. It is waged in our own lives, day in and day out, in our homes, in our work, in our school associations; it is waged over questions of love and respect, of loyalty and fidelity, of obedience and integrity. We are all involved in it—men and boys, each of us. We are winning, and the future never looked brighter ("The War We Are Winning," *Ensign*, November 1986, 45).

I was honored to speak a while back in the stake where Elizabeth Smart and her family live. Elizabeth was still missing after being kidnapped a few months before. I tried to give a good talk and offer her friends some hope. But I was more impressed with what the stake president said after I was finished. "I want to talk to you about fear," he told the youth. "The only thing we have to fear, ever, is sin." He gave a better talk than I did in only two sentences, and he was right! The only thing we have to fear, *ever*, is sin. And you know what? We don't even have to fear sin because Jesus said, "For behold, I, God, have suffered these things for all, that they might not suffer if they would repent" (D&C 19:16).

Because of repentance, our sins will be covered by the atonement of Jesus Christ. So what do we have to fear? The only thing we have to fear is *not* repenting of our sins. So let's do it; let's repent!

Temporal Lessons from the War Chapters

Because we are living in a time of wars and rumors of war, the war chapters become frighteningly real. When we see war on television and in the newspaper, we begin to understand another reason the war chapters were preserved for us. Here are a few temporal lessons from the war chapters:

1. Remember that military strength without spiritual strength means weakness. Moroni taught the Nephites to prepare spiritually before going into battle. If we as a nation skip the spiritual preparation and rely only on weapons and tactics for deliverance, we border on idolatry. President Spencer W. Kimball taught:

> We are a warlike people, easily distracted from our assignment of preparing for the coming of the Lord. When enemies rise up, we commit vast resources to the fabrication of gods of stone and steel—ships, planes, missiles, fortifications—and depend on them for protection and deliverance. When threatened, we become antienemy instead of pro-kingdom of God; we train a man in the art of war and call him a patriot, thus, in the manner of Satan's counterfeit of true patriotism, perverting the Savior's teaching: "Love your enemies, bless them that curse you, do good to

them that hate you, and pray for them which despite-fully use you, and persecute you; that ye may be the children of your Father which is in heaven" (Matthew 5:44–45). We forget that if we are righteous the Lord will either not suffer our enemies to come upon us—and this is the special promise to the inhabitants of the land of the Americas (see 2 Nephi 1:7)—or he will fight our battles for us ("The False Gods We Worship," *Ensign*, June 1976, 6).

Dwight D. Eisenhower was a general in World War II. After the success of the allied forces in Europe, General Eisenhower ran for president of the United States and won. One evening President Eisenhower invited a few close friends over to the White House. After listening to his guests discuss world events, the president commented:

> My friends, the biggest, most powerful weapon in the world is not the atomic bomb, or even the fighting ability of men. It is their moral and spiritual strength. Nothing can ever conquer that strength. Remember this, gentlemen, because that is the weapon our enemies really fear (cited in John Longden, Conference Report, April 1968, 138).

In the late 1800s, a French philosopher named Alexis de Tocqueville visited the United States, looking for what made America great. What he finally discovered and credited for America's greatness is my favorite part of the following quote, which is attributed to him:

> I sought for the key to the greatness and genius

of America in her harbors . . . ; in her fertile fields and boundless forests; in her rich mines and vast world commerce; in her public school system and institutions of learning. . . . Not until I went into the churches of America and heard her pulpits aflame with righteousness did I understand the secret of her genius and power. America is great because America is good, and if America ever ceases to be good, America will cease to be great (in *America's God and Country*, comp. William J. Federer [Coppell, Texas: FAME Publishing, 1994], 205).

The war chapters teach us that the secret to being great temporally is being good spiritually.

2. Be sorry to take up arms. War is a horrible, messy, hellish business. Moroni and the other righteous warriors felt great sorrow and reluctance in taking up arms against the Lamanites and in sending others "out of this world into an eternal world, unprepared to meet their God" (Alma 48:23). They knew their cause was just, but they were not warmongers.

I have always liked this statement from Elder Marion D. Hanks about how the Lord felt as the Egyptian armies (who were pursuing Moses and the children of Israel) began to drown in the waters of the Red Sea:

> Jewish tradition helps us further appreciate the nature of our Heavenly Father in the tender practice of the Half Hallels offered at Passover in celebration of the historic exodus of the children of Israel from Egypt and their passing through the Red Sea. When

171

they reached the sea, the pursuing Egyptian armies overtook them. Through Moses, God divided the waters, "And the children of Israel went into the midst of the sea upon the dry ground" (Exodus 14:22). The Egyptians went in after them. Then Moses stretched his hand again over the sea, and the waters returned. The Israelites were safe, and the Egyptian armies were drowning. Triumphantly the people began to sing hymns of praise to the Lord. But the Almighty stopped them and said, "How can you sing hymns of praise and jubilation when so many of my children are drowning in the sea?"

In remembrance of that event, Jewish people during the latter period of Passover include abridged or shortened psalms of praise, Half Hallels, as part of the celebration ("A Loving, Communicating God," *Ensign,* November 1992, 63–64).

I will never forget that sentence: "How can you sing hymns of praise and jubilation when so many of my children are drowning in the sea?" It seems to me that the attitude we should have about war, even when our cause is just, is one of reluctance and sorrow.

3. Elect and support righteous leaders. Captain Moroni was a righteous leader—so righteous that the "powers of hell would [be] shaken forever" if all of us could be like him (Alma 48:17). Certainly, part of our temporal preparation in this time of wars and rumors of war would be to elect good, honorable people to government office. Like Captain Moroni, our government leaders will have to make difficult decisions regarding war. President Gordon B. Hinckley observed:

> As citizens we are all under the direction of our respective national leaders. They have access to greater political and military intelligence than do the people generally. Those in the armed services are under obligation to their respective governments to execute the will of the sovereign. When they joined the military service, they entered into a contract by which they are presently bound and to which they have dutifully responded ("War and Peace," *Ensign,* May 2003, 79).

Because leaders in our government have access to greater military intelligence, we can do little except trust them, pray for them, and hope they make the best decisions possible. Because we have to place so much trust in our leaders, we should do our best to elect honorable, trustworthy people.

4. When world events get you down, let Christ lift you up. When things look rough out there, when the news is dismal, don't forget—events are unfolding as prophesied. In a way, witnessing all of the wars in the world is a testimony that the scriptures are true. Therefore, we have no need to be paralyzed by fear. President Boyd K. Packer has written:

> This is a great time to live. When times are unsettled, when the dangers persist, the Lord pours out His blessings upon His church and kingdom. I have been associated now in the councils of the Church for upwards of thirty years. During that time I have seen,

from the sidelines at least, many a crisis. Among the leaders I have at times seen great disappointment, some concern, maybe some anxiety. One thing I have never seen is fear. Fear is the antithesis of faith. In this Church and in this kingdom there is faith. So let us look forward with an attitude of faith and hope (*The Things of the Soul* [Salt Lake City: Bookcraft, 1996], 195).

Our airwaves, newspapers, and conversations are full of war. It's hard not to be depressed. But don't let the events of the last days bring you down; rather, let Christ lift you up. At the end of the Book of Mormon, a faithful father was worried that his son might have become weighed down with the wars and the killing going on around him. Notice these words from Mormon to Moroni that seem so applicable today:

> My son, be faithful in Christ; and may not the things which I have written grieve thee, to weigh thee down unto death; but may Christ lift thee up, and may his sufferings and death, and the showing his body unto our fathers, and his mercy and long-suffering, and the hope of his glory and of eternal life, rest in your mind forever (Moroni 9:25).

Carry On

I am thankful beyond words for the Book of Mormon. The people we've read about in these war chapters went through amazingly difficult times, and I'm grateful that the prophet Mormon shared these experiences with us. If the ancient prophets saw our day, they also saw wars. But they showed us how to rely on the Prince of Peace. In our day President Gordon B. Hinckley has also taught us how to build our foundation:

> This life is but a chapter in the eternal plan of our Father. It is full of conflict and seeming incongruities. Some die young. Some live to old age. We cannot explain it. But we accept it with the certain knowledge that through the atoning sacrifice of our Lord we shall all go on living, and this with the comforting assurance of His immeasurable love.
>
> He has said, "Learn of me, and listen to my words; walk in the meekness of my Spirit, and you shall have peace in me" (D&C 19:23). And there, my brothers and sisters, we rest our faith. Regardless of the circumstances, we have the comfort and peace of Christ our Savior, our Redeemer, the living Son of the living God ("War and Peace," *Ensign*, May 2003, 81).

Writing is hard work, but I have enjoyed writing this book more than anything else I've ever written. I guess it's because of the subject matter. I hope you've enjoyed it too. I'm sure that as you study the war chapters, you'll find lots of wonderful things that I missed. That's the great thing about scripture study. New discoveries await you on every page, and you can make those discoveries anytime you want because you have your own Book of Mormon.

I hope these war chapters have become a little more interesting to you. If so, then perhaps this little book did some good. Well, it's time to close—this book, that is, not the scriptures! In fact, I'm going to go open my scriptures and find another group of chapters to study. If you've stuck with me this long, I'll bet that's what you'll be doing too. So take care and keep the faith, and I'll see you in the scriptures!

INDEX